Take Charge of Your
Teaching Evaluation

JENNIFER ANSBACH

Take Charge
of your
Teaching
Evaluation

*How to Grow Professionally
and Get a Good Evaluation*

HEINEMANN
Portsmouth, NH

Heinemann

361 Hanover Street

Portsmouth, NH 03801–3912

www.heinemann.com

Offices and agents throughout the world

Cataloging-in-Publication Data is on file with the Library of Congress.

ISBN: 978-0-325-09273-7

Editor: Tobey Antao
Production Editor: Sonja S. Chapman
Typesetter: Gina Poirier Design
Cover design: Lisa Fowler
Interior design: Suzanne Heiser
Author photograph: Alyse Liebowitz / 3 Chicks That Click Photography
Manufacturing: Steve Bernier

Printed in the United States of America on acid-free paper

21 20 19 18 17 VP 1 2 3 4 5

***To Noah,** for believing that I could*

Contents

Acknowledgments

While my name is on the cover of this book, it would not exist without so many who have provided guidance, assistance, and encouragement along the way. I owe gratitude to so many.

First, my students, past and present, who continue to be the reason I do this work. To the long-ago graduates, especially Kirk and Roxane, who keep in touch and remind me that this work endures, thank you. To the students in my classroom today and tomorrow, I know you will help me find new ways to be better.

To my colleagues in Manchester and Pleasantville, thank you for the years of collegiality. P'ville friends, thank you for years of support and friendship, and despite knowing "same as ever," believing we have the power to change our students' experiences and ourselves. To my faithful friends at MTHS, thank you for all you do to help kids every day. You inspire me.

My NCTE/ALAN tribe reminds me what's possible every day. I'm honored for the opportunities to present with you and learn from you. Every teacher should be so lucky as to have a place they can always feel at home.

To my Douglass and Rutgers family, thank you for giving me something to strive for. It's an honor to be a Scarlet Knight alongside such greatness. Thank you to the American Studies department past and present for showing me a new way to see the world. Special thanks to Dr. Michael Aaron Rockland, who has provided sage advice and encouragement for more than 25 years.

Those who have come before me, inspired me, and showed me new ways to think about teaching: Kylene Beers, Jim Burke, Kelly Gallagher, Carol Jago, Penny Kittle, Teri Lesesne, Jeff Wilhelm, and more than I could ever list, thank you. Ken Lindblom, thank you for your support and encouragement to share my ideas in print.

My coconspirator, Sarah Mulhern Gross, listened to endless ideas and worries and complaints, and knew the right answer to Los Lonely Boys being the only thing that plays on the car stereo is laughter.

To the teachers who gave so much of their time in speaking to me about evaluations, thank you. Special thanks to Damien Bariexca, Steve Fence, Glenda Funk, Aracelli Iacovalli, Chris Kervina, Kelly Kosch, Luann Christensen Lee, Keisha Rembert, Stephanie Robertazzi, Lisa Sidorick-Weise, Lee Ann Spillane, Heather Staples, Denise Weintraut, and Russ Whaley.

My amazing editor, Tobey Antao, makes my ideas more focused and clear than I ever imagined possible. Thank you for your wisdom, insight, and support. This book would not exist without you. You make me a better writer, teacher, and thinker. Thank you to the talented and hardworking team at Heinemann who made this book look polished and inviting. Vicki Boyd, head of Heinemann, thank you for the work Heinemann does every day to help teachers make a difference. Thank you to Sarah Fournier, managing editor, for believing in this book. Publisher Lisa Fowler who designed the cover—thank you for bringing my ideas to life. Suzanne Heiser designed the interior of the book, making it both beautiful and useful. Production Editor Sonja Chapman shepherded a typed Word draft into this tangible form, handling a myriad of details along the way. Editorial coordinator Amanda Bondi answers more questions in a row than anyone should have to endure, and helped refine the book you are holding. And to all the people who work behind the scenes so that this idea became a book and may find its way to those who need it, including Patty Adams, director of production; Eric Chalek, director of professional book marketing; Brett Whitmarsh, director of social media; Erik Ickes, e-marketing manager, thank you for your time and expertise to make this book so much more than I could ever hope it to be.

To my association, NJEA, and the people who make it strong, especially Mike Ritzius, who provided much needed listening and advice, thank you.

National Board, the National Board process, and my fellow NBCTs have taught me so much about what it means to be a reflective teacher.

To my parents, who taught me to love learning and reading, and who pushed me to dream a little bigger my whole life.

To Noah, who sustains me and encourages me, and who has done so much in the past year to make this book possible, I can never thank you enough.

And to my sweet girl, Robin, my constant writing companion who provided us so much joy. I love you, little dog. Thank you for being our friend for so long.

Start Here
An Introduction to this Work

"My district uses the Danielson framework, and evaluators rarely spend any time in my room."

"The evaluation? It's not helpful to anyone. The system isn't uniform."

"To me, it depends on whether the evaluator likes you or not."

"My postobservation conferences last a few minutes and generally consist of 'I need a signature.'"

"Even though I've been teaching for years, it still makes me nervous when someone comes in to watch me teach."

These are some of the comments I heard from teachers as I interviewed people for this book. I spoke to teachers working in a variety of content areas all across the United States. Most spoke of evaluations and observations as something to be endured. A few felt evaluations and observations were something inflicted upon teachers. Many felt evaluations and observations were biased. And none of the people I spoke with felt their evaluations and observations were collaborative, collegial processes that helped them improve their instructional practice.

It doesn't have to be this way.

My goal in writing this book is to help you take charge of the story of your practice and your classroom, to make the most of the observation and evaluation process, and to become a stronger advocate and educator for your students.

Tell Your Story

In 2005, I attended a summer teaching institute for the humanities. Over the course of the week, the twenty-five participants grew to learn more not only about the subject matter we were studying but also about the teaching contexts that vary so widely in our state. At the time, I was teaching in one of my state's neediest districts, and I saw my attendance at the institute as a way to be certain I was doing right by my students. At the end of the week, as we were sharing ways we could use what we had learned to create new units for our students, a woman who was a supervisor at a nearby district said to me, "Wow. I didn't know your district had teachers like you. I would have hired you."

This comment stunned me. First, I realized that she assumed I was teaching in my district because I had been turned down by other districts. But I had applied only to the district I was teaching in: I had been looking for a change and a challenge. Second, in that moment I understood how the larger world saw my colleagues and me—because we taught in what was labeled a failing school district, we were failures, also.

Perhaps you have a similar story, one in which you've seen someone make an unflattering, inaccurate assumption about your work or about our profession. If so, you've likely had the same stunned reaction I had. As professionals, we care what people think of us. We want to do a good job. We want others to know we do a good job. If we want others to truly understand our work—individually or as a profession—we must take control of the stories we tell ourselves and others.

Right now, many teachers feel as though they have little control in their professional lives. The outside demands of teaching with changing standards, high-stakes tests, value-added models, teacher accountability, and increasing paperwork to document needs, remediation, and growth overwhelm even the most easygoing teachers. Evaluations can add to the stress, but they don't have to.

Instead, we can embrace the evaluation tools as opportunities to redefine how we see ourselves and our students. While many outside voices seek to label teachers as ineffective or to repair their "deficiencies," teachers themselves can instead amplify the positive work they do inside and outside the classroom.

We can see evaluations as someone else's judgment . . . or we can see them as a way for us to show what we can do. Just as we encourage our students to use assessments to showcase their learning, we need to shift our thinking about evaluations as a way to reflect on our practice and showcase our own growth and learning.

This is not to say that current evaluation models are desirable or effective or even fair. Instead, it is a reminder to focus on the parts of the evaluation we can control. When someone visits our classrooms, we have the opportunity to let them see how amazing our students are and help contextualize the learning and growth they can see there. When we are asked how we have grown as professionals, we have a chance to share our own learning and invite our administrators and colleagues to learn with us. How much of your professional self are you sharing regularly? After working alongside me for eight years, a woman who went from being a colleague in my department to my administrator was surprised to learn I peer-reviewed articles for a content-area journal. Despite years of chatting and collaborating on curriculum together, somehow this part of my professional life had not come up. We need to own those parts of ourselves as threads of the larger narrative of who we are as teachers.

Take Charge of This Year's Evaluation

The late, influential educator and researcher Donald Graves reminded us, "There is no greater energy giver than an effective evaluation. . . . There is so much art in teaching that every conscientious teacher is usually aided by another set of eyes and a strong listener" (2001, 142). Many teachers have supervisors who approach the evaluation process with this sense of collegiality, offering another view of the teacher's classroom. However, many teachers I have spoken to do not see the evaluation process as a collaboration, and some are intimidated by the process and therefore don't speak up about how it might be more effective or more equitable. They feel that evaluations are situations in which they are judged, situations in which they have little control. I'm hopeful that this book will help you to make your evaluations more effective by making them more collaborative. Together, we'll navigate the evaluation process so that you can clearly present yourself, your teaching, and your students' growth so that evaluators can see the strong work you are doing.

Graves wrote, "Perhaps people have forgotten we are a profession because we have not fought hard enough on behalf of the children" (2001, 149). Connecting ourselves back to our purpose—our students—keeps us invigorated and focused on our goals. This book is a guide for setting your own course for change this year, steered by your own professional needs, the needs of your students, and the advice of your administration. Understanding our strengths helps us know what we do best in our classroom to help students. Acknowledging what we need to change or improve, while scary, is also key to helping our students. To do our jobs well means constantly increasing our own capacity to teach students what they need to know, whether that's learning new content or discovering ways to design our classroom for student ownership and motivation.

This book is also about learning. I hope that this year you'll find ways of staying rejuvenated in and out of the classroom by creating a learning plan for yourself that goes beyond mandates. We spend our days as dispensers of information and architects of others' learning; wrestling with new concepts and skills reminds us of what it is like on the other side of the desk.

Finally, this book offers a reminder that you are not alone: we've all been there, had that day, watched that lesson flop. Together, we can learn from each other. Teaching is often a solitary endeavor in the midst of many, many people—students, colleagues, administrators, parents, and even the local, national, and international media. Education talks about collaboration, but when it comes to evaluation, things are done quietly behind closed doors, with few sharing what is in those evaluations. By sharing ideas about what the process can look like and offering suggestions for how to frame your teaching, this book can take away some of the mystery of evaluations.

To be clear, this book is not a list of tricks to improve your evaluation score, although there are strategies here that will help you connect your practice to the evaluation tool better. The goal of this book is not to help teachers who are not interested in growth or student learning game the system or skate by without doing the work. Even the most masterful teacher can grow in some way. This book offers ways to document the thinking and planning that go on behind the scenes. Working through this book will help you to focus your instruction on your students and to implement your own plans for deepening your understanding of your content area or of pedagogy.

How to Use This Book

This book follows the structure of the school year. Chapter 2 starts with a self-inventory that can be completed even if you don't know what district you'll be working in. Chapter 3 unpacks the evaluation rubric; your evaluation model will be available even if your teaching schedule is released late in the summer. Then, once you know what you'll be teaching, you can use Chapter 4 to map the curriculum to your goals and needs. Once you are in the classroom, you'll meet your students, and Chapter 5 discusses ways to get to know them and their needs better. Most districts offer an announced observation first, so the evaluation cycle begins there in Chapter 6 with the preobservation conference documentation. The remaining chapters trace the evaluation process through the end of the year—completing the announced observation, planning for and working through the postobservation conference, adjusting your own plans for the year as a result of the conference,

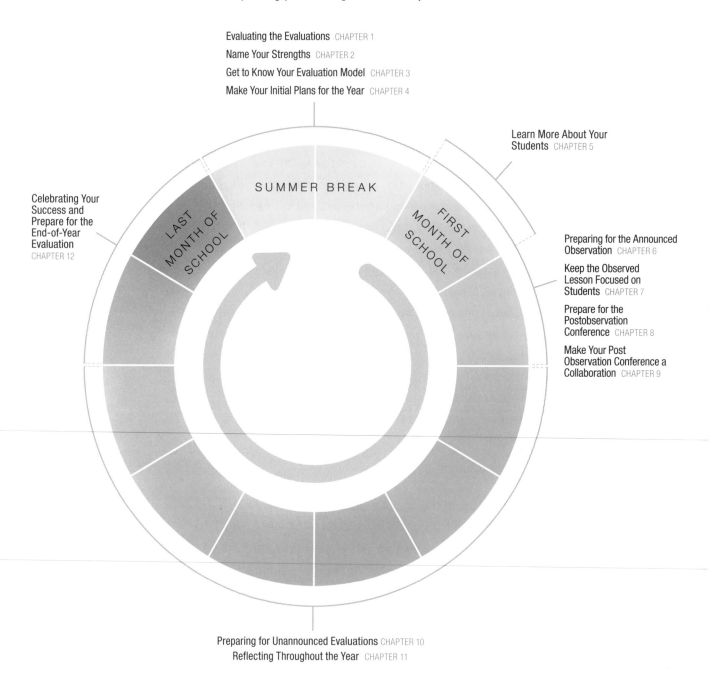

Evaluating the Evaluations CHAPTER 1
Name Your Strengths CHAPTER 2
Get to Know Your Evaluation Model CHAPTER 3
Make Your Initial Plans for the Year CHAPTER 4

Learn More About Your Students CHAPTER 5

SUMMER BREAK

FIRST MONTH OF SCHOOL

LAST MONTH OF SCHOOL

Celebrating Your Success and Prepare for the End-of-Year Evaluation CHAPTER 12

Preparing for the Announced Observation CHAPTER 6

Keep the Observed Lesson Focused on Students CHAPTER 7

Prepare for the Postobservation Conference CHAPTER 8

Make Your Post Observation Conference a Collaboration CHAPTER 9

Preparing for Unannounced Evaluations CHAPTER 10
Reflecting Throughout the Year CHAPTER 11

planning for and working through future observations, and presenting your work for the end-of-the-year evaluation.

Of course, if you are not picking up this book over the summer, you can jump into the chapter most relevant to your needs to get immediate advice and read the earlier chapters to round out your understanding when you get a chance.

The Book Within This Book: Your Professional Development Journal

This book is an interactive guide to help you chart your own course for the year. In the chapters, you'll find dozens of reproducible pages. These pages are designed to help you build a journal for planning, reflecting, and gathering evidence across the school year. Printable PDFs of the same pages are also available online at www .heinemann.com (see access instructions below). This book also provides guidance for collecting your own artifacts, examples of student work, and evidence of planning in your journal. Of course, you should feel free to modify anything to meet your needs. This is a way of organizing how you think about your practice and is not intended as additional required paperwork.

Accessing Online Resources

To access the printable Professional Development Journal online resource pages for *Take Charge of Your Teaching Evaluation* go to **www.heinemann.com** and click on the link in the upper right to **Log In**.

If you do not already have an account with Heinemann you will need to create an account.

Register your product by entering the code: **TEVAL**

Once you have registered your product, it will appear in the list of **My Online Resources.**

Professional Journal Pages Included in This Book

This journal will help you to see your own growth and to make decisions based on what is best for your students and for you as a professional. It will also give you the materials you'll need to show your growth and professionalism across the year. I use this kind of journal as a basis for the Domain 4 binder that I am required to provide as part of my own evaluation within the Danielson model.

Working through the book this way means that you'll be prepared, even in an unannounced observation, to bring evidence of your professional work with you to your postconference, allowing you to lead the conversation to your strengths, goals, and learning. This work is a great reminder of just how much you do on behalf of your students and how much you learn each year as you grow professionally. But, most importantly, it's a tool to help you grow professionally and to do a better job— for yourself and for your students—year after year.

Evaluating the Evaluations

Before we consider our own evaluations and how our own practice and expertise fit into the requirements of a particular system, we may gain some helpful perspective by considering the forces at work in our field as a whole and the origins of our current evaluation systems. In her 2014 book on the history of American education, *The Teacher Wars*, Dana Goldstein reminds us, "The history of American public education shows teachers are uniquely vulnerable to political pressures and moral panics that have nothing to do with the quality of their work" (230). We can be less vulnerable if we know a bit more about how our evaluation systems have been shaped by today's pressures and panics. In this chapter we'll explore the current emphasis on "best practice" and the myth of our failing schools as they relate to teaching evaluations. We'll also consider the costs of today's climate and evaluation systems to teachers and students.

The Emphasis on "Best Practice"

At the heart of all useful teacher evaluation work is the question of what good teaching is. It's also a question that every teacher seeks to answer. Good teaching is often hard to define because the students vary from place to place, year to year, class to class. Sometimes teachers put together what they think meets the criteria for "good teaching," and it succeeds in one class period and flops in another.

Many researchers have attempted to define what good teaching looks like. Most agree it begins before the students enter the classroom, as the teacher starts planning. However, over the past twenty years, the term *best practice* has become a buzzword in education, with few stopping to question it. Who has defined these best practices? For whom are they the best practice? Under what learning conditions? There is a push to standardize instruction that conflicts with personalization of instruction. Teachers need to push back and question how we arrived at these *best practices*.

The Limitations of "Best Practice"

As educators, we need to take time to make sure we are using strategies that are effective, and research helps us make strong decisions. However, as Rutgers University Graduate School of Education professor Bruce Baker (@SchlFinance101) cautioned in a November 2, 2016, conversation on Twitter, "the search for 'best practice' is . . . most often a doomed one. [It l]acks flexibility." Baker, who studies educational policy and finance, noted that when looking at best practice, researchers have a tendency to study the same strategies and contexts over and over, "leaving large gaps in what's known." Meta-analysis and meta-meta-analysis, then, only compound this issue and give more weight to studies that may have been flawed in the first place. In a book review of *Surpassing Shanghai: An Agenda for American Education Built on the World's Leading Systems* (Tucker 2011), Jay P. Greene, a professor of educational reform at the University of Arkansas, states, "'Best practices' is the worst practice," and goes on to explain how research that looks only at successful practices does not consider the variables that make them successful, lacking "scientific credibility" (2012, 72). He states that it continues to be a "path to fame and fortune" (72) and adds, "There is a reason that promoters of best-practices approaches are called 'gurus.' Their expertise must be derived from a mystical sphere, because it cannot be based on a scientific appraisal of the evidence" (73). Indeed, there are many gurus in education peddling best practices and teaching methods that somehow get codified into must-do practices. Some of these gurus and corporations sell whole solutions to educators, who buy them and implement them with an almost religious zeal. However, if these solutions were so simple, wouldn't most of the problems in education be solved by now? Perhaps our practices need to be more varied and customized to our students and their needs rather than based on a checklist.

A Close Look at One Version of Best Practice

The "findings" of one proponent of a version of *best practice*, John Hattie, have made their way into checklists published in education magazines that trickle down into classrooms, administrative directives, and evaluation criteria, sometimes added on to the rubric of the adopted evaluation model. Let's take a close look at where those findings came from.

In 2009, Hattie, a New Zealand education professor, released **Visible Learning**, his book on the "synthesis" of over eight hundred meta-analyses, which attempts to name best practices. Instead of conducting research himself, Hattie used a statistical formula to determine the "most effective" teaching strategies. While Hattie has many devotees, a cautious look at his methods gives pause. In one review, German professor of education Ewald Terhart (2011) finds several significant shortcomings in Hattie's book, including the omission of qualitative studies and the lack of discussion of how studies were chosen for inclusion. Hattie (2009) himself said he was not concerned with the quality of the studies. Another study raises many of the same concerns. "Any meta-analysis that does not exclude poor or inadequate studies is misleading, and potentially damaging if it leads to ill-advised policy developments" (Snook et al. 2009, 94). Most of the studies in Hattie's book are several decades old (from the 1980s and 1990s). Further, just because Hattie is linking student achievement to certain practices, Terhart (2011) notes, it doesn't mean that there is causality. Hattie, both reviews point out, does not consider social backgrounds, inequality, racism, or issues of school structures in student achievement; his sole focus is on teacher behavior to the exclusion of everything else.

Among Terhart's criticisms of *Visible Learning* is that Hattie is advocating a teacher-centered, teacher-directed form of teaching, "which is characterized essentially by constant performance assessments directed to the students and to teachers" (2011, 434). Terhart continues, "This *Americanization* of the New Zealand classroom suppresses creativity of teachers and their teaching methods, having been developed in a very bottom up-manner in the practical field of teaching" (434). In addition, Hattie specifically condemns constructivist methods of teaching, which puts him at odds with current beliefs about how students learn.

And yet, Hattie's work, as translated into checklists and short articles, has been accepted by many administrators as "best practice" and used as a guide for giving direction and feedback to teachers. And, like Marzano, Hattie also sells an evaluation system that champions the ideas in his books.

"Best Practice" that Becomes Evaluation Criteria

There's a history of attempting to define *best practice* in the United States, as well, and some of these suggested best practices become codified into evaluation requirements. Robert J. Marzano, working at the Mid-continent Regional Educational Laboratory (McREL), also did work in meta-analysis, combining multiple studies through a mathematical formula to determine the "most effective" strategies. In 1998, he published *A Theory-Based Meta-Analysis of Research on Instruction*, and in 2000 he and Barbara B. Gaddy and Ceri Dean published *What Works in Classroom Instruction*, which outlined what they claimed were the nine most effective strategies in instruction—in essence, an attempt at defining *best practice*. His methods have shortcomings similar to Hattie's work: instead of conducting their own research, they combined existing studies using a formula to determine what would be most effective, again without considering the demographics, training, or intent of those studies (among other variables). Marzano ultimately created his own company, Marzano and Associates, and continues to publish books and articles on what works in classrooms. Many of these publications are still seen as best practice today, and ultimately inform his own evaluation model.

The What Works Clearinghouse

If you're looking for educational "programs, products, practices, and policies" that have been evaluated based on "high quality research" (rather than meta-analyses), the What Works Clearinghouse (WWC), established in 2002, is a valuable tool. The WWC defines its stringent standards for considering studies as valid and includes studies on the efficacy (or lack thereof) of a variety of popular programs. This online database, developed by the Institute of Education Sciences (part of the U.S. Department of Education), offers those making decisions about education, including parents, teachers, administrators, and policymakers, access to vetted studies and conclusions about what works.

The Myth of Our Failing Schools

Several times a year, it seems, some "study" comes out that purports that America's schools are failing and clamoring for reform. However, most of the studies lack scientific rigor. In 2016, Professor Bruce Baker and Mark Weber published a paper titled *Deconstructing the Myth of American Public Schooling Inefficiency* in which they argue that the diversity of the U.S. educational system, including high poverty and moderate to larger class sizes, makes it difficult to find comparable nations because the country essentially has fifty-one different educational systems. States like Massachusetts and New Jersey score competitively on international tests, but schools in areas with fewer resources and high poverty, such as Florida, do not.

However, many billionaires (and foundations bankrolled by billionaires) have bought in to the myth of failing schools while funding and endorsing policies that require many school districts and states to buy solutions to these "problems" from a number of companies that make millions of dollars from these government contracts.

Research Professor of Education Diane Ravitch (2014) sees the move to discredit public schools and teachers as part of the push for privatization, to put public school monies into the pockets of private providers who are held to lower standards of accountability. Ravitch writes, "The schools are in crisis because of persistent, orchestrated attacks on them and their teachers and principals, and attacks on the very principle of public responsibility for public education. These attacks create a false sense of crisis and serve the interests of those who want to privatize the public schools" (xi). Those wanting to privatize public schools include well-funded players. The Bill and Melinda Gates Foundation, for example, funded both Common Core and the push to change teacher evaluations, continuing to call America's public schools "failing" (Strauss 2015).

It is this failing-schools argument that continues to drive policy for education reform, again, with solutions for sale. But how did this myth take root and grow?

In 1966, the U.S. Office of Education issued a report, *Equality of Educational Opportunity* (Coleman et al.), generally referred to as the **Coleman Report**, after head researcher James S. Coleman of Johns Hopkins University. This paper investigated the equity of educational opportunities for students in America, paying particular attention to issues of race. In that report, which clearly delineated the inequities of the American education system, teacher education and preparation was one measure of comparison.

In 1983, President Ronald Reagan's National Commission on Excellence in Education released *A Nation at Risk: The Imperative for Education Reform*, a report steeped in Cold War fears that called our schools failing and touched off the wave of reforms that continue today. It identified students and teachers as the problem. The majority of the commission consisted of administrators, with only a single teacher. Unlike the Coleman Report, *A Nation at Risk* did not address issues of poverty, racism, or equity. While other studies of the report came to radically different conclusions and attempted to refute some of the points made, they were not given much press. The public perception of teachers and students as ineffective and lazy began to take hold.

The **No Child Left Behind Act**, passed in 2002, mandated public schools build in accountability with the annual testing of students, and it required teachers

The National Board for Professional Teaching Standards

Interestingly, the National Board for Professional Teaching Standards—the organization that offers National Board Certification and encourages student-centered practices—can also trace its origins to *A Nation at Risk. A Nation Prepared: Teachers for the 21st Century,* a report released in 1986 by the Task Force on Teaching as a Profession, funded by the Carnegie Forum on Education and the Economy, was a response to *A Nation at Risk.* This report called for the formation of a board to define expectations of teachers. The National Board for Professional Teaching Standards formed in 1987 and, in 1989, published a policy statement, *What Teachers Should Know and Be Able to Do.* This became the foundational document of the NBPTS (revised in 2016), outlining five core propositions (not specific best practices): (1) teachers are committed to students and their learning, (2) teachers know their content and how to teach it, (3) teachers are responsible for managing and monitoring student learning, (4) teachers think systematically about their practice and learn from experience, and (5) teachers are members of learning communities.

The standards for the NBPTS outline what teachers do but not how they achieve those goals, allowing maximum flexibility for teachers to meet the needs of the students they teach. This is in stark contrast to the current push to evaluate teachers, which is much more prescriptive.

to be "highly qualified" (although it left states to define that individually). In 2009, the New Teacher Project, started by former Washington, D.C., schools chancellor and endorser of the failing-schools myth Michelle Rhee, released a report titled **The Widget Effect** (Weisberg et al. 2009). It calls for systems of evaluation that "differentiate teachers based on their effectiveness in promoting student achievement" (7). The report begins from the notion that it is problematic that most teachers are currently rated "good or great." Instead of trusting the scores that teachers earned, the authors of *The Widget Effect* insist that the scores must not be valid, which again suggests a presumption of failing schools. "Student achievement" (7) is left undefined except to mention "student assessment" (27). The report also calls for administrators to be trained in teacher evaluation models and held accountable for their implementation, for these evaluations to be used to determine "teaching assignment, professional development, compensation, retention, and dismissal," for it to be easier to dismiss teachers who are ineffective, and for streamlining due process laws.

The Widget Effect includes a section on value-added models, known as VAMs. "These models," it explains, "use various predictive factors to determine how well students are expected to achieve on standardized tests and then measure the positive or negative variation from that expected performance level as a means of evaluating the impact of individual teachers" (27). So, VAMs attempt to determine how much of a student's score is because of the "quality" of the teacher. The report offers no evidence for the efficacy of VAMs, and many policy and education experts, including the American Statistical Association, consider VAMs a flawed system.

Also in 2009, President Barack Obama announced the **Race to the Top** grants. To be eligible for the grants, states adopted new teacher evaluation models and included student achievement in teacher assessments. The grant criteria borrowed heavily from *The Widget Effect*.

As a result, by 2015, only five states did not require student achievement as part of teacher evaluation (Doherty and Jacobs 2015). At the same time, the assumption that there were many ineffective teachers who were achieving deceptively high scores on their evaluations persisted: the National Council on Teacher Quality, a think tank created by the conservative Thomas B. Fordham Foundation, claims, "There is a troubling pattern emerging. . . . The vast majority of teachers—almost all—are identified as effective or highly effective" (Doherty and Jacobs 2015, 3). Interestingly, Charlotte Danielson, best known for her Framework for Teaching model, drew very different conclusions when she examined teachers' evaluation results. Instead of agreeing with assumptions that the positive scores were inflated, she found that the small number of teachers who were labeled ineffective each year was inflated. She determined that many of those who had been labeled ineffective were, in fact, excellent teachers. However, they had challenged the status quo while making changes to help students succeed (2016).

The MET Project, funded by the Bill and Melinda Gates Foundation, argues in its final findings report in 2013 for the new teacher evaluation reforms in general. It endorses the use of "achievement gains," or VAMs specifically, despite there being significant studies proving their unreliability. In a blog post, Baker (2013) calls the foundation's focus on VAMs "arrogant" and "wrongheaded behavior."

Another study of the new teacher evaluation systems concluded that the relationship between value-added models and observer ratings was weak (Morgan et al. 2014), which coincides with a report by the National Center for Education Evaluation and Regional Assistance (Ruffini et al. 2014).

A separate study on the legal ramifications of the new teacher evaluation requirements found that the new evaluation systems, with their arbitrary cutoff scores, could place teachers in the wrong level of effectiveness 35 percent of the time (Baker, Oluwole, and Green 2013).

In her 2014 book *Reign of Error*, Diane Ravitch deconstructs issues with current educational policy and argues that American public schools are not broken. She notes that some economists say student families have the biggest impact on student learning, with families contributing to 60 percent of student achievement, teachers accounting for perhaps as much as 15 percent, with the total percentage attributable to the school as a whole somewhere between 20 and 25 percent. So while teachers may be the largest single factor in a school, they are significantly less important than many other factors (102–103). Yet the current climate continues to pigeonhole teachers as responsible for the whole of education, and for the individual success of each student on their rosters, regardless of circumstances.

We must, then, remember that if we don't advocate for ourselves, there will be no one left to advocate for us—or for our students.

The Costs of Today's Evaluation Systems

Many of the teachers I spoke with about their experiences echoed what recent studies about the current evaluation models say: the evaluations take up too much time and require significant paperwork for both the evaluator and the teacher. In one study of teacher perceptions of the new system in my home state of New Jersey, researchers concluded, "In theory, a teacher evaluation system should measure a teacher's strengths and weaknesses through an accurate and consistent process that provides timely and useful feedback. . . . Measuring teacher performance is complicated and there is no formula for what makes a good teacher, which means there is no formula for what should be included in the evaluation" (Callahan and Sadeghi 2015, 49). This argument points out one of the major concerns of the evaluation system: districts (or in some cases, states) decide on a single model, based on a belief system of what good teaching is, which by definition restricts what constitutes good teaching, regardless of teaching context, student background, or teacher experience.

The study goes on to discuss the differences between measuring teachers and developing teachers—two very different processes that we attempt to combine into a single system. In making a determination of a teacher's performance, the evaluator makes it difficult to focus on coaching specific areas of improvement because so many other elements need to be included in the evaluation. The study noted that as the number of evaluations increased, the teachers reported a decrease in how fair and how helpful the evaluations were because the new system is too scripted and formulaic, and evaluators were spending more time entering data than observing. It can be difficult to be aware of an entire classroom when the focus is on typing everything up on a tablet or laptop. The authors summarize that "teachers in New Jersey are demoralized, and one of the contributing factors is the emphasis on rating teachers. We need to move beyond checklists and rubrics that fail to recognize teaching excellence and we need to identify and offer professional development strategies that are most effective to improving teaching pedagogy and ultimately improving student achievement" (57).

Finally, Race to the Top required states to blend both new evaluation models and student achievement scores to get teachers' final ratings. However, a 2015 study (Hewitt) of North Carolina teachers who worked with a blended model found that teachers found the process unfair and felt an increase in stress, pressure, and anxiety. Competition began to replace collaboration. Teachers left the field. And there were uglier results, as well, from teachers who feared poor scores: Some began to make test results the focus of their work. Some actively tried to avoid students or schools that might result in lower scores.

Scholar Doris A. Santoro (2011) argues that the current climate of testing and accountability requires teachers to teach in ways that go against what they know "to be good and right (ethical and moral)" (5) by not meeting student needs, and this causes them personal distress. Santoro notes that the conversations we hear about "teacher burnout" are ways to frame teacher struggles as personal failings rather than reveal problems with the larger practice of teaching (9). The implied message is that if teachers budgeted their personal reserves better, they would not burn out. However, Santoro claims that teachers are suffering not from burnout but from "demoralization." She asserts that most educators teach because they want the "moral rewards" of teaching, such as helping our students succeed and meeting their needs in the classroom. "Unlike burnout, which suggests the exhaustion of an individual teacher's personal resources, demoralization comes from a teacher's inability to access moral rewards in the practice of teaching" (12), leading teachers to feel discouraged and depressed.

Ultimately, the increased paperwork and measures to ensure accountability are costing American schools dearly. The increased accountability demands cause teacher turnover, especially in those districts that are struggling (Ingersoll, Merrill, and May 2016), and the lack of veteran teachers hurts student achievement. A longitudinal study by Ronfeldt, Loeb, and Wyckoff (2012) examined the effect of teacher turnover over a ten-year period on 1.1 million students in the fourth and fifth grades. It showed "a direct effect of teacher turnover on student achievement. Teacher turnover has a significantly negative effect on student achievement in both math and ELA," with the worst effects on the lowest-performing schools (21–22). The study showed negative effects not just on the students of the replacement teachers but even on the students of teachers who did not leave, suggesting that a loss of collegiality or institutional knowledge also plays a part. Keeping experienced teachers in classrooms is one of the best ways to ensure student growth.

Speaking up for ourselves is speaking up for our students. The standardization of testing and instruction is hurting students. As educators, we need to use our voices to protect our students and ourselves from systemic demoralization.

Today's Evaluation Models

To understand how the models work, it helps to understand where the models came from. In doing so, we can better understand the limitations of these models, especially when they are used rigidly.

In the 1970s and 1980s, Madeline Hunter's **Direct Instruction model** listed seven elements of effective instruction. By the early '90s, many teacher preparation programs relied on her model as a standard for how to structure lessons. However, Hunter herself felt that the model was misunderstood. In a 1985 article, she explained that the model was not designed to evaluate teachers, but to help pinpoint where improvement could be made. Hunter pointed out that not every element belonged in every lesson. This is in stark contrast to the checklist mentality the model inadvertently sparked. She went on to say that administrators should not seek to make teachers apply the model in the same way they used it but to allow teachers to make it their own (60). This is a common complaint from teachers I spoke with about how the current evaluation models are being used, as well, suggesting this is a larger issue with supervision and evaluation.

The links between the elements of instruction Robert Marzano touts as best practices in the **Marzano Causal Teacher Evaluation System,** his **2017 Marzano Focused Teacher Evaluation Model,** and the Hunter model are clear and, as Baker noted, show the shortcomings of best practice.

According to Marzano's résumé, which he included in his application for the Brock Prize and which is available on its website, he taught in New York City schools from 1967 to 1968, received his BA in English from Iona College in June 1968, and worked as the chair of an English department in Seattle from 1969 to 1971. He finished his MA in education in June 1971. He left high school teaching after that. His ideas about teaching come from his meta-research, not from extensive classroom experience. Nor do they come from rigorous research he conducted in classrooms but instead from preexisting research, which he analyzed and turned into checklists of "best practice."

In a 2014 interview, Marzano said he created his model of instructional evaluation to be much more specific than others available, with forty-one different elements and strategies within those elements. He added that this model is meant to develop teachers, not measure them, and "if you are going to measure teachers—if that is the goal—then you aren't going to observe all 41 elements of the model. There are a number of models that measure teachers, and those have anywhere between 10 and 15 things that raters look for" (14). However, the Marzano Causal Teacher Evaluation System (2014 protocol) has four domains and sixty total elements, although the website states districts can focus on only a few strategies a year (however, it appears teachers are evaluated on more than two or three elements each year). His new 2017 Marzano Focused Teacher Evaluation Model whittles these down to "twenty-three essential teacher competencies." While the classroom observations are considered formative assessments for the teacher, they are included in the final evaluation of the teacher, which results in a measure of teacher performance. This seems to conflate the development and measurement of teachers and exceeds the ten to fifteen things Marzano said raters should look for.

The **McREL model** consists of five domains and twenty-five elements. Its software is designed to incorporate "student achievement" (such as test scores) into teacher evaluations. In addition, this model is based on the McREL book

Classroom Instruction That Works, which Marzano wrote with Debra Pickering and Jane Pollock (2001) when he was at McREL. As a result, there are some overlaps in ideas, although with twenty-five elements instead of sixty, the McREL model is less detailed. McREL claims that this model both measures teacher achievement and develops teacher growth.

James Stronge's **Stronge Teacher and Leader Effectiveness Performance System** is another model used throughout the country. It consists of seven performance standards and forty-eight performance indicators. Stronge, a College of William and Mary professor and head of Stronge and Associates, also incorporates student achievement into his model, although in a presentation to the New Jersey Principals and Supervisors Association in 2012, he admitted that due to the margin of error, the summative rating is "a bit artificial" and that a teacher's summative rating couldn't reliably be predicted (Mooney 2012).

The **Danielson model**, one of the most widely used in the country and modified or adapted by many states and districts, has four domains and twenty-two components, although current drafts on the Danielson Group website group the components instead into six clusters. Danielson taught for a few years in Washington, D.C., although her online biography does not say what her position was. She spent most of her career working for Educational Testing Service (ETS). Her model is based on her *Framework for Teaching*, first published in 1996, and she founded the Danielson Group in 2011. At the 2012 Educational Forum of New Jersey, Danielson said that she created the model to help teachers reflect and improve their teaching, not to evaluate teachers. In a 2016 issue of *EdWeek*, Danielson argues that despite the best of intentions, the attempts to define good teaching and distill it into policy have fallen short: "I'm deeply troubled by the transformation of teaching from a complex profession requiring nuanced judgment to the performance of certain behaviors that can be ticked off on a checklist. In fact, I (and many others in the academic and policy communities) believe it's time for a major rethinking of how we structure teacher evaluation to ensure that teachers, as professionals, can benefit from numerous opportunities to continually refine their craft." Perhaps by adding her voice to the growing number of education policy critics, Danielson will help change the course of teacher evaluations, as many of the claims she made for her system, including that it was objective and consistent from evaluator to evaluator, are the very things studies (Ruffini et al. 2014; Callahan and Sadeghi 2015; Riordan et al. 2015) show teachers and evaluators are refuting.

All of the evaluation systems generate a profit for the companies who sell them, and the companies also offer (and often require) training at an additional cost, software platforms, and additional resources. And remember the **New Teacher Project**, the organization that published *The Widget Effect*, which Race to the Top borrowed heavily from? Well, that organization also has an evaluation model for sale.

There's Work to Be Done

The new laws that govern teaching have been framed by many as having "unintended consequences." However, in an article analyzing how mainstream media, education journals, and arts education journals discussed Race to the Top and teacher evaluations, Professors Carla E. Aguilar and Lauren Kapalka Richerme urge educators to see the resulting teacher evaluation systems as intentional, hoping that in defining them that way, teachers "may better understand their own potential role as policy creators and challengers" (2014, 118), becoming involved in the process of shaping policy whether through running for school boards or speaking up and advocating for better policies for student learning.

Taking charge of our teaching evaluations is another way to fight back. We can refuse to be demoralized by a system that may not have our best interests (or our students' best interests) at heart. We can even use the evaluation system to show our strengths, our professionalism, and our focus on our students' needs. The evaluation process, regardless of the usefulness of the feedback we are given, offers a way to build a habit of reflecting on what works in our classrooms. From that place of self-knowledge, we can advocate for ourselves, our students, and our profession.

Clearly, there's work to be done. Take a deep breath, and let's get started.

2 Naming What You Bring to the Classroom

In my first year of teaching, I brought tremendous energy to the classroom. When the students asked if we could read "real books," I set up student-driven book clubs, where students chose whom they wanted to be in a club with and what book they wanted to read. When they wanted to know more about *The Great Gatsby*, we made it a class project, with students researching different aspects of life in the 1920s and then teaching their classmates. We celebrated with a Gatsby-inspired party. Teams of students handled different aspects of the party: The decor team turned the school library into an Art Deco speakeasy. The food team served "champagne" (ginger ale) in plastic champagne glasses. The entertainment team taught partygoers how to do the Charleston and taught classmates jokes and slang of the time period. Students each role-played the part of someone from the 1920s, either an individual of their own creation, a historical figure, or a fictional character, including Gatsby. Students who took that class will remember the 1920s long after everything else we studied that year fades.

So what did I see as my strengths then? A willingness to take risks, to put in long hours, and to let students take the lead. Those qualities still mark my teaching. But back then, I didn't have the experience to help students make deeper connections to all of our readings. I let them create book clubs, but I had no idea how to make the clubs part of the regular classroom. I didn't have a classroom library to help them discover the readers within themselves. But I passionately wanted them to love reading as much as I did. While I know these students engaged deeply with the content and knew the time period well, this activity did not make them stronger readers.

Before we get our first teaching job, and before we set foot into a classroom for a new year, we can step back and look at our strengths. We will look at the evaluation rubrics in the next chapter, but before we attempt to measure ourselves by anyone else's rubric, let's take a moment to consider who we are as individual teachers. We are not interchangeable parts, and we need to honor our own strengths, personalities, and unique talents. What do we offer students? While the current educational climate often refers to standardizing learning, the fact is, each teacher brings gifts to his or her students, and thinking about those helps us design class-rooms and learning experiences that bring students further in their learning. By looking at what I could do well, I started to see places where I could grow as an educator. I sought out books such as Jim Burke's *Reading Reminders* (2000) and Jeffrey Wilhelm's *You Gotta BE the Book* (1996) as I looked for ways to increase student engagement with literature.

As teachers, we're not often required to consider our strengths and areas for growth. Certainly, in job interviews we can talk about ways to engage students and design lessons and assessments, but that is not the same as taking a step back to think about where we found the most success, or what sparked us to change a practice, or how students pushed us to grow and learn from them or find new ways to guide them. The late educator Donald Graves wrote that another way to consider what you do well is to ask yourself what you like best about teaching. "Usually," he explained, "your competency comes at the point of what you genuinely enjoy doing" (2001, 22). So consider this a way to think about what we love about our work. Inventorying accomplishments and strengths helps frame what we do as teachers positively. Looking at our own experiences and skills helps us move forward as the designers of our students' experiences. Teaching involves so many demands and forms and records that sometimes we forget to consider what we love about what we do and focus on why we do it. When we take a moment to think about where our content knowledge lies and how what we learn could help our students, we rein-vigorate ourselves. We begin to see possibilities for ourselves both as learners and as leaders. Most importantly, we find our way back to our own curiosity and energy.

This chapter offers you an opportunity to do some professional—and personal—reflection. If you have a chance to do this before the beginning of the school year, when you are not juggling all of the day-to-day details of classroom life, you might find it easy to think about these long-range questions with an open mind. If you're coming to this work midyear, while part of your mind is still working out next week's lesson plans and you're eyeing a pile of papers to grade, you might want to give your-self a quick break before working through this chapter. Let yourself clear your head, if only during a quick walk around the block, to help you focus on your work as a whole, not just the work of this week.

The sections that follow will prompt you to consider your experience, your strengths, and your goals. You can capture your thinking on the reproducible pages at the end of this chapter or in a separate document, either of which can then be added to the binder you're building for your evaluation work.

It may be tempting to think that this step isn't completely necessary for preparing for your evaluation. After all, there isn't a box to check off on the evaluation rubric for this kind of highly personal reflection, is there?

While it's possible that no evaluator will ever ask to see these notes, they are foundational for the work you'll be doing this year. When we don't keep our own strengths and goals firmly in mind in our work, when we let the points on an evaluation rubric become our only guiding lights, we lose track of what is best for our students and for our own growth as professionals. If we are in this profession for the long haul, we must take ownership of our work. That ownership begins here.

Our past experiences inform how we see ourselves, our students, and our surroundings. When we frame our experiences in a positive light and focus on what we do well, we see our students and ourselves more generously. When we accept a deficit model of professional development, we take on the beliefs that we are lacking in skills and require remediation—a stance that will not help us to grow or to take risks. Professional researchers are not less accomplished because there is more research to be done; likewise, we are not less competent because there are new methods and skills that we can bring to the classroom. Taking time to establish who we are as teachers gives us the benefit of the doubt when needed and helps us choose our path forward.

See Professional Journal Page 2.01 at the end of this chapter for a reproducible note-taking form.

(Also available online as a digital download.)

Think of a Time When You Felt Successful

Whether you planned a unit that kept students engaged and reaching beyond what you originally envisioned, taught a lesson that hit your objectives, or made a connection with a hard-to-reach student, stop and think about what success has looked like for you in your classroom. How do you know you succeeded? This question lies at the heart of improving our practice. How do we know what we know? What evidence do we have? When we consider evidence to be about more than test scores, we understand that anecdotal evidence, running records, small changes in student behavior and outcomes make a difference and should be considered.

For example, a student who told me in the first week of school that he had no interest in books and spent the first month of class trying to nap eventually discovered Andrew Smith's *Grasshopper Jungle*. The strange narrative held the young man's attention as he was forced to build new reading skills. It took him a month to get through that book. When he finished, he asked for another. My regular book talks and classroom library of over 750 books intrigued him. Soon, he was devouring books, keeping his "Books to Read" list updated in his notebook and ignoring his other classes to engage with new stories. My reading program draws heavily on Penny Kittle's *Book Love* (2012) and Donalyn Miller's *The Book Whisperer* (2009), allowing me to use student-selected texts to increase student's reading ability. I fed him a steady diet of books that challenged his reading, whether through different genres or background knowledge required or complex narrative structures. If I were to look at his grades, I'd see they did not show progress. He refused to write about what he read or complete assignments. However, if I thought about how he began to see himself differently, how he began to see his life differently, I could measure progress. At some point, some twenty-five books or more into his journey, he let it slip that he loved the stories he was reading (Andrew Smith's books best of all) because they showed him that no matter what you come from, you can make a way for your life as an adult. The power of this floored me. And yet, I had nothing to record in any data sheet that showed my success in helping this young man grow as a person, to consider his circumstances in a new light. Take some time to think about your successes, and celebrate that they represent your accomplishments, too.

Think About a Time You Helped Another Teacher

When have you shared your skills with a colleague? Did someone ask you for ideas for a project? Look to you for book recommendations? Wonder how he or she could integrate technology into his or her classroom? Perhaps you showed someone how to use a feature in the online grade book. Whatever it is, use it as a way to see your skills through another lens. Often, we don't give ourselves enough credit for what we know, and we assume everyone can do it. When we step back and see how we have helped others, however, we can appreciate that we have knowledge or skills that are important in our jobs as teachers. I had a teaching colleague who made the best unit binders—she could arrange everything so that her plans, handouts, formative assessments, board notes, and summative assessments were all there with tabs so that at a glance, anyone could see the map of where she was going with any unit. I asked her if she could show me how she put the binder together and we looked through a few while she explained her process, which she thought was obvious. While I have never mastered her technique, her demonstration has informed the way I conceive of units ever since.

Consider a Time You Changed Your Practice

What adjustments have you made to improve your teaching? Maybe you went to a workshop or a conference and heard someone speak. Perhaps you saw a colleague in action or received a suggestion from a supervisor on another way you could do something. How did you go about making this change? Maybe you searched Pinterest for a picture of what you wanted. Maybe you found a book that detailed what you were interested in learning. What experiences led you to moments of growth and change? Seek more of those out.

I know teachers who are constantly redeveloping their lessons without leaving their home; they spend time on Twitter and read blog posts for ideas, engage others in conversation, and work through new ways of seeing what they do.

Reflect on the Results of a Change You Made in Your Practice

Again, consider *how* you know what the results of your teaching are. Where did you see changes in what students produced or the processes they followed to get there? How did your students feel about this change? How did you feel? Look for positive moments to build upon. Sometimes changing something as simple as a handout to look at things from a new perspective makes the difference. Don't get bogged down in whether the change was big enough—look for times when even small adjustments helped students excel.

Consider a Time Your Students Helped You Grow

What did you learn by watching students or from soliciting their feedback? Years ago, I used a predictive study guide to help students. Some students found the guide helpful. However, the stronger readers asked if they could modify the assignment so that it didn't interrupt their reading. I realized I could build in more opportunities for students to take the lead on their learning. My students taught me that they can be trusted to choose what is right for them.

Think About a Time Students Asked More of You

Students might ask for more from you directly or through their actions. What did they need from you? Could you recognize it at the time? How did you meet their request? Years ago, before diversity campaigns in young adult literature were getting widespread exposure, I was teaching in a school where 99 percent of the student body was made up of students of color. However, the textbook we had reflected predominantly white authors, we didn't have classroom libraries of trade paperbacks for students, and the school library's holdings were outdated and not diverse. When we talked about the literature, students had difficulty connecting to it or seeing how it was relevant to their own lives. The students didn't directly ask me to find more relevant texts for them, but I could see that they needed texts that spoke to them more directly. I sought out professional development courses online in what was then referred to as multicultural literature, made a case to my superintendent for funding new texts, and developed units on topics relevant to my students.

Consider Your Philosophies on Student Learning and the Teacher's Role

How do your ideas about the ways in which students learn and educators should teach fit with your approach to teaching? Even as preservice teachers, we are often asked to explain our educational philosophy. Our ideas about teaching should change as we grow and gain more experience, and as we modify our practice, sometimes we need to step back and think about what this new way of doing things says about what we believe. If we believe school is a place to develop citizens, for example, we should be incorporating skills for participating in democracy in the classroom. If we believe our primary job is to prepare students for a world that does not yet exist, we might focus more on helping students break down tasks to be more self-directed and self-sufficient. Ask yourself, "How am I making myself obsolete for these students? How am I helping them to do valuable things without my assistance?"

Remember Your Passion

We all entered education for a reason. Some of us wanted to inspire a new generation or to share our passion for our subject area or to give back to our communities. Some of us just want

`2.02`

See Professional Journal Page 2.02 at the end of this chapter for a reproducible note-taking form.

(Also available online as a digital download.)

to work with young people. Others want to empower students to be change agents themselves. The day-to-day realities of teaching, however, often make us feel far removed from why we wanted to do this. Let's stack the deck, spend some time reconnecting with what we are doing, and establish some reminders to return to when we need a lift.

What Do You Love About Teaching?

Why do *you* teach? Take a moment to focus on the important work you do rather than the job you do. I love those moments when students make connections that I didn't see, when they are thinking deeply about something and are so engaged they complain about how quickly the class has gone. Special education high school mathematics teacher Janine Affuso-Duffy says she loves "watching a student who comes in in September with an 'I can't do math' attitude change over the course of the year into a student who exits [her] class in June confidently saying, 'I *can* do math!' and firmly believing that." Special education high school history teacher Lisa Sidorick-Weise focuses on how her students grow: "When you get to see the leaps and bounds—that's the happiness."

What Are Some of Your Favorite Teaching Moments?

Think of special moments that have stuck in your mind over time. The bulletin board over my desk, which we call the wall of fame, is filled with sticky notes of various shapes, sizes, and colors. Throughout the year, when a memorable moment happens or someone says something quotable, either I or a student memorializes it on a sticky note and adds it to the wall. Spending a few moments now and then catching up on what was shared in that class and across my classes helps us all laugh and remember that we are in this together.

What Do You Love About Your Position Specifically?

What is great about your particular teaching circumstances? Do you have a classroom that lets you watch the sun rise every morning? Are you tucked into a quiet corner or in the middle of the action? How have you made the physical space your own—for example, by bringing in a variety of chairs and organizing conversation spaces to help students learn? Think about the roles you play and the content you teach or the freedoms you have. Maybe you teach an elective you love or maybe you can create your own reading list. All positions have drawbacks; focusing on the positive helps keep your energy positive, too.

What Do You Love About Your School and About Teaching There?

Think about what makes your school special. For me, supportive colleagues make the difference between just getting through the day and enjoying my work. Having teaching peers who share materials and ideas freely helps not only with the workload but with feeling invested in a community. Are there particular traditions that you look forward to each year? Faculty talent shows, winter ice cream socials, schoolwide read-aloud celebrations, student fairs with student-run demonstrations of learning—all of these things shape the culture and climate of a school community.

What Do You Love About Your Teaching Space?

Think about what you like about your classroom. Perhaps you get latitude in how you arrange your room or what furniture you may use to create the learning environment. Maybe you, like teacher and author Lee Ann Spillane, have the space, freedom, and funding to create more options for students to choose where to sit, allowing them to take more ownership and feel part of the classroom. Of course, not all teachers have those luxuries. Think about the space you share with your students. What makes it special?

What Do You Love About Your Students?

Now consider your students. Do you love their friendliness, inquisitiveness, compassion? Make notes about the things you love so you can create opportunities for your new students to show you the same.

What New Memories Do You Hope to Make This Year?

Whether you are looking forward to the homecoming week activities or creating a classroom with student-run discussions, setting positive expectations can give you a place to return to when the inevitable daily frustrations set in.

Analyze Your Practice and Consider the Year Ahead

Each September, the school year seems to stretch on to eternity, and its possibilities appear infinite. Yet, by January, most of us are wondering where the time went and how we will fit everything in. Taking a moment now to outline what you hope to accomplish and to start planning how to make that happen will provide a road map

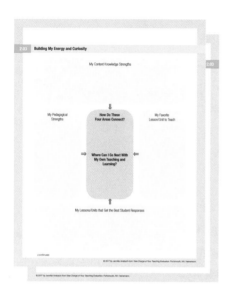

See Professional Journal Page 2.03 at the end of this chapter for a reproducible note-taking form.

(Also available online as a digital download.)

to your destination. You may need to change routes along the way, but you'll need a plan to start your journey. Let's begin by taking an inventory of your strengths.

What Areas of Your Content Knowledge Are Strongest?

Perhaps you have read extensively about Wordsworth or Joyce and can not only analyze the texts but offer background knowledge of their biographies to flesh out details and draw connections. Or you might be an expert on Alexander Hamilton, having read multiple accounts of his life, including the perspectives of his contemporaries. You might be a fellow in a university teacher fellows program, having spent summers in the field alongside researchers to learn the latest on not only what is known about a specific area but how the knowledge was acquired and what comes next. How have you built this content knowledge? How did you most enjoy learning it? Sometimes we forget to see ourselves as learners. We owe it to our students to keep ourselves in mind and be aware of our own learning preferences, if only to remind ourselves that our students might feel differently.

What Are Your Most Effective Teaching Methods?

How do you teach best? How often do you use those methods? How do they fit with your philosophies of students, education, and learning? Take a moment to examine how your classroom experiences reflect your strengths in teaching methods. To do that, **think about your favorite lesson, unit, or text to teach.** What draws you to it? Then **consider what lesson or unit gets the best response from students.** How do you know it gets the best response? Consider how you are measuring both *best* and *response*. Is it level of engagement and participation? How well students remember it later? How well students perform on assessment tools? Sometimes we get caught up in measuring and forget to consider what the purpose of the measurement is.

Where Do Your Passions, Your Strengths, and Students' Engagement Intersect?

What are the points of connection between your interests, your strengths as a teacher, and your students' interests and strengths as learners? Where can you make more connections? This is the essential piece of what you are currently doing and where you might go next with both your teaching and your own learning.

What Beliefs and Ideas Are Holding You Back?

Is there anything keeping you from doing better work? Perhaps you read a blog post about someone's classroom and thought, "My students could never do that." Or maybe you worry that you don't have the skills to make your idea work, that your students don't have enough resources, or that your kids don't have the right background, the right mind-set, the right community. While it is important to be realistic about your school community and its resources, it's also important to be mindful of where your thinking is holding you back. Changing our beliefs is challenging and often scary, without question. But if we let our beliefs hold us back, we never consider all the possibilities for ourselves, our classrooms, or our students.

How Can You Grow Your Content Knowledge This Year?

What steps could you take to feel confident enough to try something new? For example, I wanted to improve my approach to teaching diverse texts, rather than just make them available. Over the past eight years, I sought out booklists of diverse texts and read them voraciously, keeping track of how they lent themselves to teaching literary elements and author's craft. Because I was interested in diversity, I sought out resources through Teaching Tolerance (www.tolerance.org), from the Southern Poverty Law Center, where I found several webinars on how to evaluate texts for diversity. This increased my content knowledge and helped me address contemporary issues I knew my students cared about.

What New Methods, Tools, and Strategies Could You Try?

What can you implement that you're not currently using? Math teachers might want to experiment with student-created flowcharts, for example, to show decision making in problem solving and to reflect the diverse ways to arrive at an answer. History teachers might decide to explore how to incorporate anchor charts into teaching students how to reason arguments. A forensic science teacher I know made arrangements for staff from the county prosecutor's office to come to class and talk about how forensics are playing a role in their area, since not all jurisdictions have access to the resources and equipment students see on television. A colleague who teaches business invited a local entrepreneur with a popular restaurant chain to talk about how to create and expand a business.

What Would You Would Like to Learn for Yourself This Year?

Whether it's a skill such as how to cook something, or it's information such as the role science played in the Cold War, plan to learn something for yourself. Take a moment to put yourself in the role of learner and decide whether you would enjoy taking an online class, joining a group at the library, finding a seminar to attend, or reading books on the subject. Keeping ourselves challenged and growing helps us stay in touch with ourselves as learners, and it also helps us remember to prioritize our own well-being. Not everything we do needs to translate to the classroom, and planning to make time for things we enjoy matters to our energy levels, too.

Keep Track of It All

What tools do you currently use to capture your ideas about how lessons or units are going, what you would change next time, and what new ideas or strategies you'd like to try?

Keeping track of our great ideas ("I should do that next year!") and our reflections ("This worked well for all but period 2, who needed the lesson chunked differently because they were overwhelmed.") in a concrete way relieves our minds of this cognitive load and allows us a way to track our own progress and possibilities. We start the year energized with a plan for the year ahead and with a way to retrace our route later on.

I know teachers who blog regularly about their teaching and use it as a way to preserve their thoughts on how a lesson went and what they might change for next time. Other teachers keep a journal or jot it down in their planner. I often take notes directly on the lesson plan itself and keep the plans in a binder for reference. I also use a planner where I keep both my personal and my professional reflections. Keeping them organized makes it easy to find what I want. How well are your strategies working? What kinds of ideas might you want to track this year? Is your current method allowing you to find what you need later? What strategy or tool might be helpful to try this year?

Keep Students First

Taking time to think about ourselves may seem counterintuitive to keeping our students first, but we need to know ourselves to know what we have to offer our students. Modeling lifelong learning and how to be a learner is an important gift we give to our students. It also keeps us in a learner's mind-set, reminding us what it feels like to try something we don't think we've completely mastered. While many teachers won't try something in their classrooms unless they know they have mastered it themselves, learning alongside our students is powerful. Show them how to problem solve when things go wrong. Demonstrate how to seek answers to questions as they arise. Research with them when you aren't certain of things. Let yourself be uncomfortable and show students how to handle the discomfort that comes with being in that space of learning before mastery.

I felt successful as a teacher when . . .

I helped someone else with
his or her teaching when . . .

I changed my practice when . . .

. . . and it helped students learn by . . .

A student showed me
how to grow when . . .

A student asked more of me when . . .

. . . and I met their request when I . . .

My philosophy about how students learn and the
teacher's role is . . .

Self-Reflection: My Passion for Teaching

Favorite Teaching
Moments

What I Love About Teaching

What I Love About My School

What I Love About My Students

What I Love About My
Teaching Space

New Memories I Hope to
Make This Year

What I Love About My Position

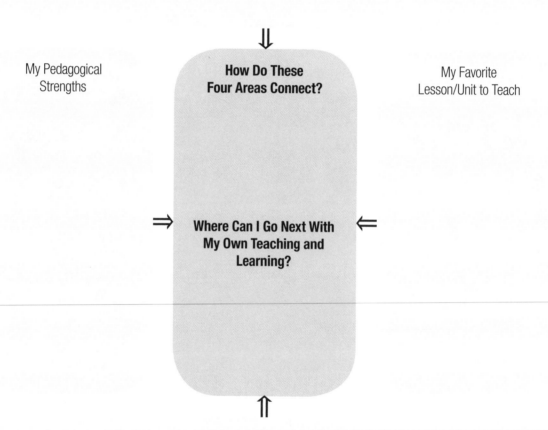

My Content Knowledge Strengths

My Pedagogical
Strengths

**How Do These
Four Areas Connect?**

My Favorite
Lesson/Unit to Teach

**Where Can I Go Next With
My Own Teaching and
Learning?**

My Lessons/Units that Get the Best Student Responses

Learn These New Things in
My Content Area:

Keep Using These Tools for Capturing,
Organizing, and Finding Ideas and Strategies:

Consider How I Can Better Track These Ideas:

Learn and Implement These New
Methods, Tools, or Strategies:

Try Using These Strategies or Tools for Capturing,
Organizing, and Finding Ideas and Strategies:

Learn This for Myself:

31

Unpacking the Evaluation Model and Creating a Road Map for Success

One day, as my class was discussing the scoring rubric for an upcoming standardized test, a sharp student raised her hand. "This is the same rubric we've been using since seventh grade," she said. I conceded that, yes, she had seen it before and waited for her to ask why I was wasting class time going over something they already knew. Instead, she showed insight into the problem of standardized rubrics.

"Well, if the rubric is the same, why do we have to keep taking the test? If we did well in seventh grade, won't our scores be just as good if we write the same thing now because it's the same rubric?"

And in that moment, I realized I needed to unpack the rubric with the students and show them the exemplars for different grade levels as well as different levels of performance. The next day I had packets made for small groups of students to share and pass around. I asked students to keep track of what they noticed that was the same and different in the various exemplars. Students left knowing not just what the rubric said but also what it would look like in practice to score at each different level.

We can do the same thing with our teaching evaluation rubrics.

To be successful by an outside standard, we need to take a moment to unpack the rubric and consider where we are in relationship to the standards being defined. In doing this, we build our confidence while finding specific areas for growth and considering the path we will take on our own journey. In analyzing how we already meet and exceed expectations, we also give ourselves space to pursue areas that we have not focused on before. We create a way to both explore new possibilities and reflect on those explorations: What are we studying? How are we are learning it? How we are applying what we are learning? We consider the strengths we identified in the previous chapter as they relate to the specific areas of evaluation models and then look for places we can improve, using previous evaluations as a guide to how others perceive us. When we disagree with how we have been evaluated in the past, we can focus on how to best present those aspects of ourselves going forward.

Unpacking the evaluation rubric also helps us to understand the belief system that underpins the evaluation model. A 2014 study (Goodwin and Webb) looked at how teachers fared when the evaluation model was at odds with the teachers' belief systems about how students learn. The Danielson model, for example, has a constructivist view of teaching and learning. Goodwin and Webb's study asked two questions—"What is teaching?" and "What is learning?"—and determined that many teachers in the study did not hold constructivist beliefs about teaching and learning. Marzano and McREL both endorse more direct instruction paradigms of teaching and learning. It is essential that we take the time to look at the inner workings of the evaluation model and work to address our own gaps in understanding about the expectations put forth by that model.

We must also consider how states and districts have modified these models, reduced the number of elements being scored, or weighted each element. Even if two teachers in different districts are subject to the same evaluation model, their experiences and the technical aspects of how it is applied might be different. In addition, you might also need to navigate the different teaching standards that are applied to different districts or states.

This chapter will look at the most popular models (Danielson, Marzano, McREL, and Stronge). If you are not being evaluated with one of these models, don't worry. You will be able to apply your own evaluation's criteria here or use the categories as general guides to best practice, relying on research on what makes strong teaching and the National Board teaching standards as other reference points. A review of the models adopted by different states shows that most are modifications of the Danielson model, so if you are not working with one of the models discussed here, that may be a good place to start.

Get to Know Your Evaluation Model

It's worth noting that different evaluation models promote different skills. Achieving the highest-level score requires showcasing different skills for different models, even if many of the skills required for other levels of effectiveness are similar; that is, a teacher who is considered highly effective under the Stronge model may fall short in the Danielson model. Here are a few brief sketches of what some of today's major evaluation systems seem to promote.

Danielson: The language that describes the "distinguished" level includes words like *thorough, extensive, accurate, specific, regularly, variety,* and *fully* (Danielson 2013). For example, the difference between a proficient lesson and a distinguished one is that the first is "designed" while the second is "well-designed." Another key attribute of the Danielson model is that moving to distinguished teaching means more of the classroom activities and discussions are student-initiated rather than teacher-initiated. If you are working under the Danielson model or an adaptation of it, you will want to take time to think about how to move students to these levels.

Marzano: In the Marzano Teacher Evaluation Model (2013) (sometimes referred to as the Marzano Causal Teacher Evaluation Model), the highest level of proficiency, "innovating," differs from the passing level of "applying" in that the teacher "adapts and creates new strategies for unique student needs and situations" (15). A teacher under this Marzano model will need to look for ways to refine or create new material consistently. Under this evaluation system, one strategy is to identify a few students or groups that are unique early in the year and gauge how to adjust or create lessons for those students. Marzano also states that "innovating" teachers are "recognized leaders in this activity." Documentation of this might include collaborative planning documents, agendas from presentations or workshops you have given, or emails in which you shared information with others. Notes on conversations with other teachers to show leadership might also be useful.

The 2017 Marzano Focused Teacher Evaluation Model streamlines this into twenty-three elements, and now each element has a focus statement, a statement of the desired effect, and lists of evidence for both the planning and the implementation of the elements. The focus between "applying" and the top tier of "innovating" is that the "innovating" level is defined by a teacher who "helps others" (2) for some elements, and for other elements, "implements adaptations to achieve the desired effect in more than 90 percent of student evidence" (5), where the "applying" level says "the desired effect is displayed in the majority of student evidence" (5). A list of possible adaptations is included for each element where this is a criterion for "innovating." Example techniques for tasks such as "instructional techniques" and "monitoring learning" (5) are also included in some elements. This model has the potential to be interpreted as the examples given being the only examples accepted, as the rubric has checkboxes for each technique used.

McREL: The McREL system (Williams 2009) states that the highest performance level, "distinguished," is set apart from "accomplished" primarily through the teacher showing initiative and encouraging students to take ownership of their learning. This level also states that a teacher "encourages and advises others" on how to accomplish tasks. For this model, you should keep records of self-initiated professional development to show that you sought it out. In addition, collaborative planning documents or emails that show "encouraging and advising" are useful, as are notes of conversations with colleagues.

Stronge: Like the Danielson model, the Stronge model differentiates between "effective" and "highly effective" by using modifiers such as *actively, consistently, continually,* and *variety* (Stronge and Associates 2016). This model also expects the teacher to teach students how to be engaged and how to take ownership of their own learning. Unlike Danielson, it does not look for students to initiate events. The Stronge model requires teachers to provide specific artifacts and evidence of professional growth. The model stresses that teachers should maintain this evidence throughout the year.

While there are some overlaps, no two systems seem to have the exact same priorities. I highlight these differences as a reminder: if we want our evaluations to truly reflect our efforts, the ways in which we explain our good work to administrators must align with the specific rubric they are using to evaluate us. This does not mean that we take students' needs out of the equation when we are considering our work in the upcoming year. It means that we need to meet (and articulate how we meet) these requirements *while* we do what is best for our students.

Participate in District Training for Your Evaluation Model

Most likely, your district provided initial training in your evaluation model. The quality of these trainings seems to vary widely, and even the best training often needs more follow-up and reinforcement.

Many teachers I spoke to said they did not feel the training they received was adequate or useful, yet many did not take the step of analyzing the rubrics on their own. While several were discouraged because they felt that the evaluation model was applied unevenly or unfairly, I encourage you to do the work of knowing your rubric so you can clarify expectations when you are observed. If nothing else, being able to measure your own growth in your ability to help students learn is a worthy goal outside of being evaluated.

On the other hand, some districts have made the evaluation process the primary driver of professional development, helping teachers focus on improving their practice with the goal of improving student learning. Luann Christensen Lee, a National Board–certified chemistry teacher, explained that her district needed to develop a new evaluation system as part of the district's No Child Left Behind waiver. About twenty-five professionals representing the different schools in the district, union association representatives, instructional coaches, and administrators created a teacher-learning council that meets monthly to create evaluation forms and protocols. The district received a state-funded collaboration grant that addressed evaluation, assessment, and grading practices. While the end result might not be what everyone had hoped for, it allowed teachers a voice in looking at how the evaluation models work and gave them opportunities to discuss what teaching should look like.

Perhaps your training involved watching exemplar videos, practicing scoring, working within study groups, attending lectures, or trying peer evaluation. Or perhaps your district's training was minimal. No matter what situation you're in, you can make the entire process run more smoothly for you and for the observer if you take time on your own or with colleagues to unpack the language of the rubric and use that language in your pre- and postconference artifacts as well as in your observation lesson. If you are a member of a teaching union, check with your local to see if there are online or in-person workshops or tool kits to help you better visualize what the rubric calls for. Ideally, studying alongside the administrators who will be observing you will allow you to develop a shared set of expectations with them so everyone knows what different levels of performance look like in the classroom.

Unpack Your Rubric

Many of the teacher evaluation rubrics are overwhelming: lists of domains and indicators and extensive descriptions of performance levels, often with additional documentation offering examples for each of the different indicators. When I first saw the Danielson scoring rubric, I remember thinking that there was no way I could keep all of it in my mind, a feeling that was compounded by remarks from the trainers that it would be unusual to achieve the top level of performance. While some evaluators insist that they don't give 4s or have quotas for how many a person can receive, that is not the intention of the rubrics. After all, if the rubric designers didn't think the top performance were achievable, it wouldn't exist. The key is to unpack the rubric, examine the expectations and differences in shades of performance, and prepare to achieve the highest level of performance.

For those teaching special needs students, keep track of what your students can do when they arrive and what you help them learn to do throughout the year.

3.01

As you unpack the rubric that will be used to evaluate you, keep track of the differences in language across the levels in a chart with four columns: the indicator or section you're commenting on, your notes about level 3 (or whatever the passing performance level is), your notes about level 4 (or whatever the highest performance level is), and examples (we'll get to the examples later). Professional Journal Page 3.01 is a blank chart you can use, and Figure 3.1 shows a filled-in example. While cutting and pasting words into an electronic document might be helpful because your final notes will be searchable, I prefer to take notes by hand, as it forces me to process each word. I find that my recall is stronger after handwriting the notes as well.

See Professional Journal Page 3.01 at the end of this chapter for a reproducible chart to help you take notes on your rubric.

(Also available online as a digital download.)

As you make your notes, what patterns do you notice? What does your evaluation rubric prize? What, according to the rubric, makes the difference between effective teaching and excellent teaching?

Now, take a moment to look over what the level 2 (or whatever is just below passing) performance description says to note what the focus is for the indicator. For example, in the Domain 3d indicator from Danielson, a basic level shows "students appear to be only partially aware of the assessment criteria used to evaluate their work, and few assess their own work." (2011, 64). This tells us that under this evaluation system, we need to be certain students know the evaluation criteria well and that they are used to self-evaluation. You may want to note these distinctions on your chart as well.

Once you have your chart complete, go back through and read the examples given for each level. In your "Examples" column, first jot down things you already do that look like the top score. Then, perhaps in another color, go back through the examples given and jot down what you *could* do to meet that level. Staying with the assessment indicator example, if I were using the Danielson model, I would make a note that I need to teach all rubrics to students, have students help create rubrics, and teach them to apply the rubrics or complete reflection sheets on their own regularly. Forcing yourself to go through this process will help ensure you have a clear idea of what the model values and how to best present your teaching to achieve the highest score.

If you are teaching special needs students, you can also keep track of what students could do when they arrived and what you have helped them learn to do. For example, Lisa Sidorick-Weise, who teaches in both inclusion settings and special education pullout replacement history, or resource room, classes, prides herself on teaching her inclusion students to be more independent so they know when to get up and get an outside resource to help them or when it is OK to ask a friend for more information. When it comes time for observations, she has plenty of information to share that shows growth because she took notes on what they initially couldn't do without prompting and what she had to model for them.

Create Your Action Plan for the Year

Once you have the chart of your own ideas, you can begin identifying areas for growth. Look at the places where you noted what you *could* do to meet the highest performance level for the indicators. Is it something you already know how to do and need to implement, or is it something you need to learn more about to be able to implement effectively? If you already know what needs to be done, are there resources you need to create, such as student self-evaluation forms?

Create your action plan with four columns: a note about which indicator you're addressing, plus your notes about what to do, to make, and to learn (a chart is provided in Professional Journal Page 3.02). If you already know your students, consider how these plans fit with their needs. For the things you need to learn, you may know already where you can find more information or you might need to do some research to create a strategy. Now, look back at the notes you made in Chapter 2 concerning your goals for the upcoming year. Add those notes to the chart. Prioritize any activity that you need in order to show growth over previous evaluations (even if they were from a student-teaching experience, and even if you disagree with what was perceived as a weakness). The evaluator will look for these in your first observed lesson, and you want to be ready.

3.02

Be mindful of the particular requirements of the highest level of achievement in your evaluation model. For example, under evaluation models such as McREL, to earn the highest level of performance, teachers need to show they are keeping up on research and sharing with other teachers. If that were part of my evaluation, I might take some time to do a quick search relating to a couple of units (targeting ones in the months I'd be likely to be observed, if possible) and create a sharable document with the ideas I found. If my administration required me to save or print what I read, I'd do so and include it in my professional development journal. I would also note the article information and my thoughts about how I might use it in my professional development log (see Professional Journal Page 3.03). If I had time, I might even explore ideas for a unit or two to show I added new strategies or content, or I might find a short article I could give students to build background, create interest, or make connections to what they already knew.

See Professional Journal Page 3.02 at the end of this chapter for a reproducible chart for your action plan.

(Also available online as a digital download.)

If you already know your students, consider what they will need in the coming year. It may be that their needs are already addressed in this plan. For example, if you were working with the Danielson example I mentioned earlier, you could consider instances in which it would be useful for students if you unpacked rubrics with them, instances in which it would be helpful for them to cocreate rubrics, and situations when reflection sheets would be genuinely helpful to them. Your goal is to consistently find ways to both meet the evaluation's requirements *and* meet student needs. If you don't yet know your students and their needs, you can return to this document once you know them better.

Finally, review this chart and identify three items that would best help your students improve their skills for learning or their knowledge of content. Focus on those first.

When you are finished, you will have drafted your own professional growth plan for the year. This may be different from the one your school requires, or it may dovetail nicely with your required plan. By creating this chart, you have drawn a road map to your success. Just writing it all down will reflect well in your evaluation score for professional responsibilities.

Plan Your Professional Learning

As you look at your "To Learn" column, consider and note what sources of information might be of help to you in each instance. By putting yourself in the driver's seat when it comes to finding resources for your own professional development, you're ensuring that the help you get will clearly connect to your own goals and the areas for growth you've identified. Additionally, seeking out your own PD shows your initiative, your sense of professionalism, and your dedication to your students.

If you scored below passing on an area in the past, this is a good time to look for upcoming workshops or other resources in the area of concern. For areas that you are looking to push further, the beginning of the school year is a good time to look at the upcoming editorial calendars of professional journals you read, whether you are interested in writing up your experiences and research for publication or you are just seeking information on a specific topic.

Many teachers say that because of budget restrictions, their districts won't pay for them to attend professional development or give them the release time they would need. Often, even if you can't attend in-person PD, you can access online professional resources such as curriculum guides, study guides, and lesson plans. Here are other resources to consider:

- *Edcamps, Nerdcamps, TeachMeets, and unconferences* are free, teacher-driven professional development opportunities hosted by interested people; if you don't find one in your area, you could host one! Sometimes Edcamps target a certain topic such as literacy or technology. Other times, they are completely open. The agendas are made at the Edcamp based on what people want to present.

- *Twitter* offers opportunities to learn from others, through connected conversations, one-on-one discussions, and Twitter chats. Using a hashtag (#example), participants can follow a conversation on a topic of interest and participate without following all the people in the conversation. Twitter chats are hosted by individuals, nonprofits, publishers, and other corporations and cover nearly every topic in education imaginable.

A Google search of "education twitter chat calendar" will bring up a calendar that lists the hashtag and topic of every indexed Twitter education chat by date and time in daily calendar format. New chats are started all the time and old hashtags get retired (or are too full of spam to be workable), so search for what is current. Many well-organized chats also archive the chat afterward so you can scroll through and see if it interests you. Screenshots of your participation in chats and your reflections can serve as artifacts for your participation. If you're new to Twitter, consult Heinemann's free online course, Twitter for Educators (http://hein.pub /twitterforeducators), for step-by-step guidance.

- *Facebook groups* offer educators informal professional development with like-minded teachers. Facebook groups and pages for professional associations, unions, educational companies, publishers, and many others give teachers a chance to share and to connect without needing to be online at the same time. Some Facebook groups organize around topics for study or even are moderated book study groups, and it is not unheard of for authors to be available for questions. A Google search for Facebook and the topic you are interested in will help you narrow down the options. Many education blogs also create lists of Facebook groups for educators. Be mindful of publication dates because, as with all social media, pages and groups may disappear suddenly.

- Most disciplines have *discipline-specific associations or organizations for teachers*, and many host workshops, conferences, local affiliates, and newsletters with content-specific information. Joining a professional organization helps educators keep current with issues and research in their field and connects them with like-minded teachers for inspiration and collaboration. While online organizations offer people in remote areas access, making a trip to an in-person conference can be rejuvenating and can help build your professional network.

- Many *government organizations and nonprofits* offer professional development for teachers. The National Endowment for the Humanities offers summer workshops and seminars for teachers from one to four weeks in length at various sites around the country. The U.S. State Department offers several teacher opportunities, including Fulbright awards and Teachers for Global Classrooms; symposiums in Washington, DC; and an international field experience. Nonprofit organizations such as Gilder-Lehrman and National Geographic offer summer institutes for teachers as well as online workshops and other resources. A Google search of your area of interest and "teacher professional development" will yield more results.

- *Museums and arts centers* typically include education as part of their mission and often offer professional development. Some offer online classes and workshops in addition to hands-on opportunities. The Smithsonian Institute offers a variety of professional development opportunities, including residential workshops during the summer. Check local institutions as well as those on topics of interest throughout the country.

- *College and university departments of education* often offer continuing education workshops for teachers as well as graduate programs that lead to specialized certificates beyond just graduate degrees. Many host organizations that hold education and content-specific conferences and opportunities.

PD doesn't have to come from an outside source. Here are a few ideas for how to design your own professional development:

- Consider starting a *faculty book club* online or in person with your colleagues. You can study possible texts for classroom use, books about professional development topics, or books on topics related to education, such as Jessica Lahey's *Gift of Failure* (2015) or Charles Duhigg's *Power of Habit* (2014). Many publishers offer discussion guides to help organize the meetings and give direction. The conversations that stem from these experiences help teachers grow professionally and they also build relationships between colleagues.

- Start a *wiki or webpage of resources* for yourself and your colleagues. A collaborative document that provides quick links to topics of interest can expand your knowledge of available resources and make lesson planning easier. Take time to annotate the list and offer insight into what each resource offers, and you'll have documented your reflections on how you might use the resources—a helpful artifact for your professional portfolio.

- Work with colleagues to ***explore an education issue that is important to you.*** You can explore big questions such as discipline or more specific topics, like how to best word questions (I spent a year exploring this topic with a group of colleagues who volunteered, along with a facilitator, to work together). Looking at student work samples or instructional materials together can offer insight and creativity that will help you see your own practice in a new way and help you improve your instruction. Lesson study is a powerful tool for collaborating to improve student learning.

- ***Facilitate a workshop.*** As teachers, we know that one of the best ways to become an expert at something is to teach it to others. If you have a new activity, tech tool, or strategy that you are excited about, offer to lead a workshop in your school about it to help your colleagues stay energized. When I held a Twitter workshop, I was amazed at how some of my colleagues found ways to use Twitter in the classroom, which in turn extended my own thinking about it.

- ***Organize an unconference, Edcamp, or TeachMeet*** for your building, district, or geographic area. Get the word out to like-minded educators and use your professional network to bring more people together to learn with and from. Edcamp and TeachMeet both offer help in using their formats. The benefits of sharing ideas widely brings in many more people; form a committee and take roles to keep any one person from becoming overwhelmed. Schools, universities, community centers, and libraries often will let teachers use space for free.

- ***Engage in action research in your classroom.*** Is there something you aren't sure is working or you think you could improve in your classroom? The structured inquiry process of action research can empower you to take charge of the decision making in your classroom by helping you gather and analyze evidence of student learning. Attend a workshop or online webinar or read a book or online journal articles about action research to get started. The process will help you define a research question, develop and administer tools to gather data, analyze that data, and make informed decisions about your practice.

- Read through journals in your content area and then ***write an article*** of your own. Check the calls for manuscripts in the journals relevant to your content area and look for a topic you have an interest in or have been creating new ideas for. Research the topic and then craft an article that offers your own ideas and submit it. If that feels too bold, look into becoming a reviewer for the journal. Many education journals are peer-reviewed: feedback from teachers like you helps the editors determine what the journal prints. It's enlightening to read what others are doing, and most journals ask you to review only a few times a year at most.

- ***Get involved with your professional association.*** Join your national content-area association or a local affiliate and volunteer your skills in an area you feel comfortable in. Many organizations have plenty of good ideas but not enough people to make them happen. Working alongside others in your content area, especially those in various stages of their careers, may help you find a mentor or allow you to mentor a newer teacher. The organization will also help you stay current on trends and issues in your certificate area.

3.03

See Professional Journal Page 3.03 at the end of this chapter for a reproducible chart for recording professional learning.

(Also available online as a digital download.)

Record Your Professional Learning

Regardless of which learning options you choose, keep a log of your professional development activities. You might just jot down what you did and the date, but I recommend taking a few moments to note a few key ideas you took from the experience and how you can use them in your teaching. If you took notes or participated online, you might also want to print out the transcript or put a copy of those notes with your PD log. Professional Journal Page 3.03 gives you an option for a

RECORD OF PROFESSIONAL DEVELOPMENT HOURS

Name Jennifer Ansbach   District: Manchester Twp.
ANNUAL REVIEW: (Attach relevant documentation where applicable)

ACTIVITIES	DATES	# HOURS	DOCUMENTATION
Affirmative Action	9/1	.5	Certificate
Safety/Police/Gangs	9/1	.75	Certificate
Danielson/MyLearning	9/1	1	Certificate
Faculty meeting	9/1	1	Agenda
Duties meeting	9/1	.5	Agenda
NJEA/teaching on the block	9/2	1.5	Agenda
MyLearningPlan/Oasys	9/2	1	Agenda
Faculty meeting	9/2	1	Agenda
Co-teaching Meeting	9/2	1	Agenda
Faculty meeting	9/7	.75	Notes/Agenda/Memo
Faculty meeting/SGOs	9/28	.75	Notes/agenda
Department meeting	10/4, 10/5, 10/6	.75	Notes/agenda
Website training/Lee Bruzaitis	10/10	.75	Agenda
Department meeting	10/10	.75	Agenda
In-Service Day	10/10	3	Agenda
Department-content & academic vocabulary	10/19	.75	Memo
Department meeting	11/2 or 11/3	.75	Memo
Department meetings	12/6, 12/7, 12/8	.75	Memo
Faculty meeting/PARCC training	12/21	.75	Memo
Faculty meeting/best practices	1/11	.75	Memo
Department meetings	1/24 or 1/25	.75	Memo
Grade level meeting	1/31	1	Notes/agend
Faculty meeting, discipline model	2/8	.75	Memo
Department meeting-grading	2/22 or 2/23	.75	Memo
Department meeting-common grading	3/14 or 3/15	.75	Memo
Faculty meeting	3/22	.75	Memo
Faculty meeting	4/5	.75	Memo
Faculty or department meeting	4/26	.75	Memo
Faculty meeting	5/10	.75	Memo

Faculty/department meeting	5/24	.75	Memo
Faculty meeting	6/7	.75	Memo
NEH Seminar: Cold War & Aerospace in southern CA	6/25-7/2	45	Certificate
Article: CEL Ed Leadership Quarterly	July 2016 (Oct. 2016 publication)	10	Article
Book: Take Charge of Your Teaching Evaluation	Aug-Dec	100	References list
Webinar: Rock & Roll and American Fiction	10/4	5	Certificate
Webinar: Jefferson	10/11	5	Certificate
Webinar: Teaching Whiteness	10/25	.75	Certificate
Google Level 1 Bootcamp	11/10	3	Certificate
Google Level 1 Bootcamp	11/11	3	Certificate
NCTE convention	11/17-11/20	24	Certificate
Presentation: From Aha! To Action	11/18	4.5	Certificate
Presentation: Be the Change	11/20	4.5	Certificate
ALAN workshop	11/21-11/22	13	Certificate
Presentation: Get LIT!	11/21	1.5	Certificate
Webinar: Teaching Empathy	1/10	.75	Certificate
Webinar: Home Visits	1/17	.75	Certificate
Webinar: Poetry of Rita Dove	1/19	5	Certificate
Webinar: Discussing Black Lives Matter	1/31	.75	Certificate
Webinar: Teaching Black Lives Matter	1/31	.75	Certificate
Webinar: Implicit bias	2/21	.75	Certificate
LGBTrans Issues	2/22	2	Certificate
Webinar: Langston Hughes	2/23	5	Certificate
Webinar: Equity Literacy	2/28	.75	Certificate
Webinar: JFK & TV	3/2	5	Certificate
Webinar: Black Lives Matter in Historical	3/16	5	Certificate

Figure 3.1a–b Here's a glimpse of my own professional development log. Keeping track of all of the ways I learn during the year helps with my evaluations, but it also helps me to recall and use that learning in my work.

quick list-style log to give you an overview of the year's work—a bit like a table of contents.

A digital notebook tool (such as Evernote or OneNote) or a binder (to keep all your notes and certificates together, organized by indicator) can also be useful for collecting artifacts to demonstrate what you have learned from your professional development.

As you assemble these artifacts of your own learning, file them in a way that will make it easy to show your growth at your end-of-the-year conference. Use sticky notes or annotations and label what the artifacts are and why you are including them. Notes such as "New unit plan developed this spring to meet district goals" or "Lesson plan updated this year to use new ideas from workshop" will help you later.

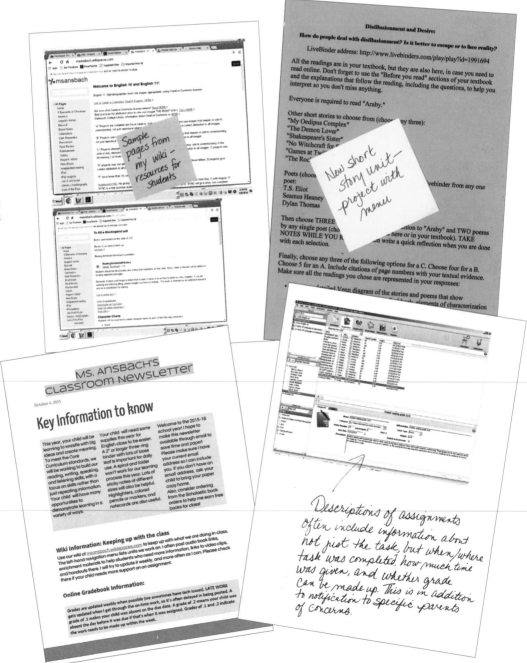

Figure 3.2a-d Gathering and labeling artifacts across the year gives you a wealth of evidence options for your evaluation.

Take Charge of Your Teaching Evaluation

Documenting Collaboration

If you collaborate with colleagues, jot down with whom you spoke and what the conversation was about to help you remember later. In addition, jot down any future dates to follow up. These informal conversations often make a big impact on your teaching because the conversations can be immediate and responsive to needs. When chatting with colleagues, we don't have to explain how school policy or culture shapes the situation—the shared experience of working in the same building allows us to get to workable solutions quickly. In addition to informal conversations, structured collaborative groups such as professional learning communities and Critical Friends Groups create minutes and artifacts that can be archived.

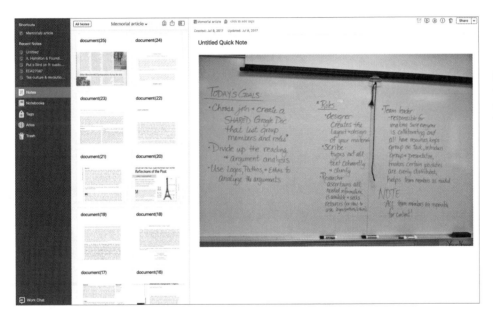

Figure 3.3 Evernote lets me keep all of my professional reading, notes, and annotations together, and it's searchable.

Documenting Professional Reading

Document blog posts, online news or journal articles, and Twitter chats with screen-shots and your own annotations. Many teachers rely on services such as Evernote, OneNote, Google Keep, or Dropbox to archive what they read along with annotations or reflections on how it might be useful. It's much more effective to save websites to folders labeled by classes or units than to save everything to a single "Teaching" folder. Even easier is to use a social bookmarking tool such as Diigo, Pocket, Google bookmarks, or iCloud bookmarks. Social bookmarks will help you collect links to tweets, Facebook posts, articles, images, and pages of websites—all with the ability to add tags and annotations to help you find what you need later. You can also highlight and share bookmarked sites with others and search for educator groups using social bookmarks to find new sites and ideas. For articles on paper, jot down the citation information and your thoughts; I sometimes also make a photocopy of the first page (or the entire article if it's short) and put it with my notes to help me remember.

Figure 3.4 Lee Ann Spillane shows that notes from a conference don't have to be boring.

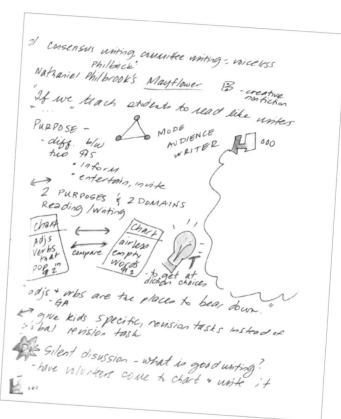

Documenting Sessions and Meetings

You can document workshops, meetings, conferences, and webinars with notes, sketchnotes (visual notes), transcriptions, or minutes. However you keep notes, they become part of the documentation of your growth, especially if you include your own reflections on what you learned.

Documenting Research

Sometimes research involves reading unit plans or lessons from others, or researching elements of your lesson such as historical photographs or video clips. Include the lesson plans to which you have added these along with screenshots of some of the resources you evaluated. It's also helpful to make notes for yourself about which items you used, which were most effective, or which you want to come back to later.

Documenting the Resources You Share

You can use screenshots of pages you create in wikis or shared documents to create a resource list for yourself or others as evidence of not only your work but your collaboration with others. Showing who shares or can edit the document will also provide evidence of collaboration. If you create materials for classroom use together, that is also helpful evidence of collaboration. Save samples of student work using the shared documents to demonstrate how this became part of student learning.

Documenting Your Published Work

If you decide to undertake writing an article of your own, keep your notes, and if you publish, put a copy of the published article with the work. If you have a draft of an article you haven't placed for publication yet, include the article with your notes and where you are considering submitting it.

Documenting How You're Using What You've Learned

In addition to evidence of your own learning, include a copy of lesson plans, unit plans, or class materials that employed what you learned along with the artifacts of your own learning. Showing how you applied the information makes the connection between your professional development and your students.

Create Tools for the School Year

Look through your "To Make" list and start creating anything that you can at this point. If you're working on this in early summer and you don't have your class list yet, you may need to think in more general terms. However, if you know what classes you'll be teaching and you have a good idea of your students' needs, you can get started immediately. If the evaluation model you are using values student record keeping, for example, begin making forms for students to mark off completed work or evaluate themselves.

This is also a good time to make yourself cheat sheets to remind you of the aspects of your practice that you want to focus on during the year. I keep question stems taped to my lectern, for example, so I can remember to use the rubric language. I find it keeps me focused and helps me to internalize the new concepts I'm working on. And, when I'm being observed, this tool helps me use the language that observers are looking for. Many people get nervous when they are being observed; if you know your mind goes blank when someone else walks into the room to evaluate, jot down a list of what you might forget and keep it where you can refer to it each day (to help to engrain the habit) and during an evaluation (when you may feel more distracted than usual). You'll find more discussion about how to prepare for observations in Chapter 6.

Taking time to create these tools now will take pressure off throughout the year. The sooner you implement using systems, for example, the easier it will be to track them and to get students involved.

Keep Students First

Unpacking the language of evaluations may temporarily—and artificially—foreground our own performance. In truth, when we focus solely on the language of a rubric or the particulars of an evaluation system, our work can feel hollow. What good is it to follow the letter of an evaluation requirement if we're not reaching our students? Thankfully, this stage is only a piece of the work we'll do across the year, and when it's done thoughtfully, it helps us to grow and to continually get better at meeting students' needs. Consider how we help students to understand how they'll be evaluated in our classes. We help students to see what's expected of them academically, but we don't limit our instruction to those expectations. We may know that a standardized test awaits students near the end of the school year, but we don't simply give them standardized test prep all year. Instead, we give them rich experiences that meet their needs, while also ensuring that they're learning what they will need to know for that test as the year unfolds. In the same way, our work here is about getting to know what is expected of us, not limiting what we will do with our students.

Rubric Criteria	Notes on the Just-Passing Level	Notes on the Highest Level	Examples

This Year's Action Plan

Section/Indicator	To Do	To Make	To Learn

Date	Event/Tool	How Can I Use This in My Teaching?	What Artifact(s) from This Professional Development Are Included in My Journal?	Corresponding Evaluation Rubric Indicator

4

Studying the Curriculum
and Planning Opportunities
to Succeed

In my first years of teaching, I often felt like I was struggling at the end of the year to squeeze everything in. A veteran teacher told me to get anything that needed to be done before June over with by December. While I have found that to be something of an exaggeration, I did learn that I needed to plan an entire year with the end in mind. Focusing on one unit at a time too often didn't leave me enough places to go. The idea of pushing everything off by a day every time we had a snow day soon proved frivolous because June teaching days—peppered with spring fever, class trips, and early dismissals—don't have the same focused time as days earlier in the year. Today, my students laugh at the fact that I can give them a clear idea of what's to come from any point in the year. I check in with them regularly, pulling my "map of time" (also known as a calendar) off the wall to remind them of what we have done so far, where we are, and where we are headed. Students are never surprised when it's time to write a research paper or read a certain book; by planning the units at the beginning, I layer in skills and procedures so that they feel that concepts build on each other. "Don't skip an assignment," one student wrote to the next year's classes. "Ms. Ansbach always has a plan, and that one assignment always becomes part of some bigger assignment, and you always feel like you should have just done the assignment in the first place."

In truth, my plan isn't quite as cast in stone as my students might think. I build my plan with the best hopes that it will be a good fit for my students, but knowing that I might need to make adjustments along the way. This could mean changing the plan to allow myself to revisit a skill that is challenging for them, fine-tuning a classroom routine, or letting their engagement with a particular topic or issue guide a unit's content focus. The clearer my initial plan is regarding what I hope to achieve, the easier it is for me to see what still needs to be addressed when I make necessary changes down the road.

My main goal in having a plan for the year's direction from day one is providing my students with the best instruction I can in the limited time I have with them over the school year. I'm sure that you've done something very like this in your own classroom, as well. However, there's another benefit to this practice that is likely invisible to my students: My plan is very intentionally aligned with the rubric with which I'll be evaluated. It includes opportunities for me to use methods and lessons that have been successful in years past, to try out new approaches, and to showcase the skills that the rubric highlights as good teaching.

Whether we're working with required, scripted curricula ("everyone will teach this page of the textbook on this day") or designing and implementing our own plans, being aware of how the days fall and where the units line up with vacations is helpful in planning. More than once, snow days and emergencies in November and December have resulted in my Shakespeare unit carrying over until after the holiday break, requiring more time for reviewing and recapping where we were and what we were working on. (I always tell students I can't believe they didn't use the extra time to review their notes daily, but, for some reason, that's never quite how they choose to use the time.)

In this chapter, we'll work together to map out a plan for the year that will address what is required by your curriculum, what your students need, what you are interested in, and what your evaluation demands of you. Thankfully, there is often much overlap between these areas.

A year-at-a-glance plan is incredibly useful for finding chunks of time and planning units of instruction. Looking at how much time you have and working backward is always the first step to planning instruction, and when you look at the year as a whole, spending a little time planning in the beginning can often save you time later as you scramble to reteach ideas because of interruptions. By mapping out and considering how units fit into the larger scheme of the year, you can better explain your reasoning for your instructional decisions and why you needed to make adjustments based on student needs.

If you're working on paper, find a one-page calendar that shows your entire school year. If you decide to work on a digital calendar, start with a fresh calendar, not one that already has

See Professional Journal Page 4.01 at the end of this chapter for a reproducible checklist to help you plan.

(Also available online as a digital download.)

your relatives' birthdays and your personal events on it—you might want to share this plan later in your evaluation process.

Now, shade in the weekends, holidays, and school closings. Note the ends of each quarter and when progress reports are due. Shade in standardized testing days, school-wide events, and anything else that will interrupt your teaching time.

Then, sit back and analyze how the time can be chunked to the curriculum. Where do you see blank days clustered together? These chunks of uninterrupted teaching time are the places for your meatiest units. Also keep in mind that days at the end of the year are often more challenging to get intensive work from students, especially if your school has a lot of field trips at that time of year. Mark off about how much time you have for each unit on this calendar, leaving a few days in each unit for unexpected interruptions, reteaching, and student energy that extends an activity (see the example in Figure 4.1). As you work, check that there's enough time between the end of one quarter and the interim progress reports for the next quarter to have enough student work to properly assess their progress.

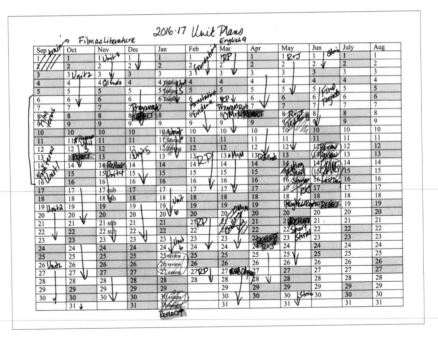

Figure 4.1 A year-at-a-glance calendar (even if it's as messy as mine) shows how much time you'll have for teaching and when you'll be interrupted by long weekends, holidays, and school events. I find it useful for chunking out units.

Begin In-Depth Planning

Once you have an overall idea of where your biggest units will fall and how many days you can devote to each unit, it's time to start planning the year in depth. For this part of the work, you'll need monthly calendars with enough space to make notations on each day. Transfer your notes about school closings and other interruptions to the monthly calendars. Note the dates when progress reports and report card grades are due. Then, add the word *reflect* on or just after those days to remind yourself to catch up on your big-picture reflections (I'll discuss these more in Chapter 11).

Mapping Time for Teaching Routines and Procedures

Start thinking through what you need to accomplish early in the year to get students ready for your units. This part of the planning reaps dividends on your evaluation. First, plan those early days to get to know students; interest and content inventories, baseline assessments of skills, and simple team-building activities help your planning and establish both a learning culture and a community in your classroom. Revisit your notes about unpacking the evaluation rubric (see Professional Journal Page 3.01 in Chapter 3), this time with an eye to what *students* need to be doing. This points the way for the skills you need to teach early in the year. For example, if the evaluation rubric says that students need to be able to explain the classroom routines and procedures, then you need to be certain that you teach them and arrange the classroom to facilitate the automatic use of those routines and procedures. Having clear procedures and routines for signing out devices, retrieving lab equipment, cleaning up supplies, and other such necessities requires time for teaching those procedures to students and time for practicing so they can do it smoothly.

Regardless of whether your evaluation model values student-run classrooms, take time to see if you can move some tasks to student responsibilities. Instructional time is at a premium, and the fewer tasks you need to do to make things run smoothly, the better. The late educator Donald Graves (2001), who taught and was a principal at the elementary level, reminded us that students can handle far more responsibilities than we often give them, and he cited tasks such as writing letters of invitation or thank-you notes as well as organizing books, class libraries, folders, and displays as appropriate tasks to delegate. He also recommended taking time to teach students how to do each task and rotating helpers so that the previous helpers can train their replacements (38). All of these suggestions will help you capture more classroom time in the long run, even if you need to spend more time initially setting up these systems.

There are a few exceptions to this teach-procedures-first rule. If you know you won't need students to be able to use a procedure until the end of the year, don't teach it in the beginning of the year because you won't have opportunities to reinforce it across the school year. You will also need to find ways to keep procedures fresh and effective after you've introduced them. For example, students may need cheat sheets to refer to, and signage in the classroom can assist with that, too. Clearly labeled "parking lots," "in-bins," student supplies, and such are helpful prompts for students. These reminders are especially helpful in, say, the second month of school, when the newness of routines has worn off—and when observations often begin.

On the monthly calendar, find the dates that you've set aside for establishing norms early in the year. Note the routines and procedures that you'll be teaching students on those days.

Planning Units: Brainstorming

Begin by brainstorming what your best teaching strategies might look like for each unit. Consider the types of **lessons that meet the highest levels of performance on your evaluation**. (See your notes on Professional Journal Page 3.01.) Note the units in which you want to do those activities. Perhaps you want to get students started with working in groups sooner, so you'll include those activities in your first unit. Maybe you want students to be able to hold Socratic seminars by the midpoint; where would be the best time to introduce those procedures? Plan to build skills on each other; for example, your expectations of their small-group discussions might be similar to the way you would like them to participate in fishbowl discussions, only with several people rather than one-on-one.

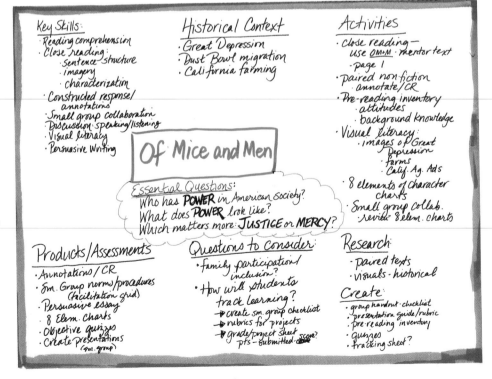

Figure 4.2 Before completely planning a unit on *Of Mice and Men*, I did this initial brainstorming, which included goals for what students would learn as well as essential questions and possible activities and assessments.

Another way to help yourself break down units is to list **parts of lessons that evaluation models require**, such as formative assessments, closures, small-group strategies, and learning games (reread your notes on Professional Journal Page 3.01 to see what you need to include). For example, the Marzano model mentions learning games specifically, and McREL cites learning games in its references. Teachers using those models should be sure they have several worthwhile learning games in their repertoire. Making notes of which of these strategies you can use in each unit will help you ensure you aren't falling back on the same one or two strategies. (See the example in Figure 4.3.)

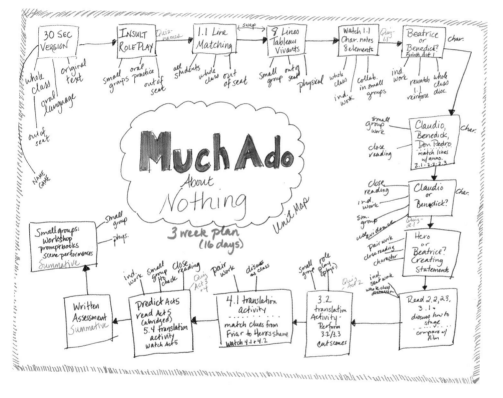

Figure 4.3 In response to my evaluation model's requirement for a variety of student groupings, my unit plan includes plans to have students work in a range of group settings that are legitimately helpful for the students and appropriate to their needs. This helps me see at a glance how well I'm moving students through the different groupings rather than relying on one or two.

Next, consider the **areas in which you'd like to show growth**. (See your notes on Professional Journal Pages 3.02 and 3.03.) Where in each unit can you build in opportunities to showcase your improvement and new learning?

Unit by unit, jot down applicable **strategies and activities that demonstrate your best teaching**. If you build each day being mindful of student needs, even in an unannounced observation, you will be able to explain the goals of the lesson, where the class is going, and how you're helping kids. Take advantage of this advance planning time to consider ways you can make engagement, student-directed learning, or interaction central —especially in units where you've felt student enthusiasm lag—while meeting the requirements of your evaluation rubric.

A story from a friend who taught art shows just how powerful engagement can be. In a conversation, she complained that her students hated lessons on lines and basics but that they had to grasp those concepts before they could work with clay in ceramics. We redesigned the unit using the principles of *Understanding by Design* (Wiggins and McTighe 2005) so that the students had to create a design for a clay pot that demonstrated their understanding of the required concepts. She gave students a week to complete the activity. Each day, she would model one of the concepts using both the chalkboard and then the clay medium so students could see how to translate the markings from two-dimensional to three-dimensional art. She could not believe the difference in student energy and engagement: what had been a unit they had to get through became a way for students to take ownership of the concept. They were not required to attend her demonstrations and were free to use textbooks or work on their sketches, but students eagerly watched her demonstrations and took notes for themselves because they needed to use the information right away.

While it's tempting to come up with a showcase lesson for each unit that offers a way for you to meet the highest levels of performance, you can never be certain that your showcase lesson will be applicable on the day of the evaluation. Additionally, your students may be bewildered during the lesson if your teaching looks dramatically different from other days. For example, in my Shakespeare units, I typically end with a performance piece. Students know we are working toward it. When I'm observed, even if the evaluator isn't there for the performance, I can talk about the unit as a whole and discuss student engagement and growth. Think about ways you can revise your planning to allow for multiple days of lessons that demonstrate your teaching at the highest levels of performance, not just a single superstar day.

Planning Units: Mapping Out Your Monthly Calendar

On your monthly calendar, sketch in rough dates for units that you established on the year-at-a-glance calendar. On the first day of each proposed unit, I make a list of the strategies I will probably use for that unit. For example, once I've completed my planning, my short story unit might say, "Focus on theme. Literary journals. Menu board projects, including imagery charts, story maps, character diary/social media entries." While this might look like a quick note, it's packed with all of the requirements we've been making notes about over the last few chapters. It includes the skill and concept I want to include (theme). It mentions the formative assessment (literary

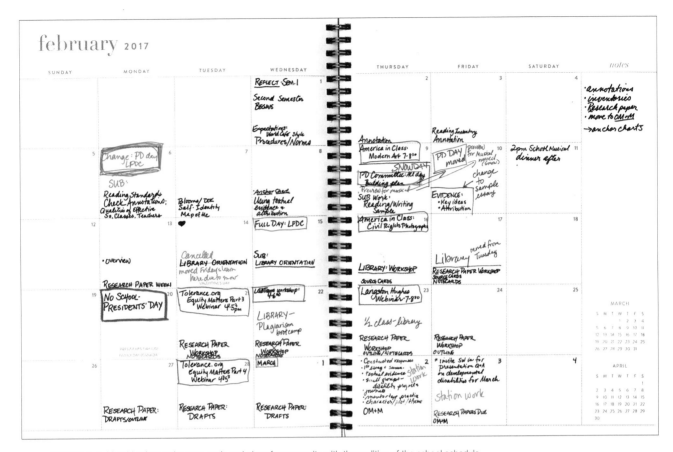

Figure 4.4 Monthly plans unite your goals and plans for your units with the realities of the school schedule.

journals) and the summative assessments, which in this case will offer a menu of options for students and still remind me that I'm working with students on imagery, plot, and character, building on those skills from earlier units. For each unit, you'll need to do some synthesizing to be sure that all of the factors you've been tracking appear in this plan.

Planning units across the year is a valuable reminder of just how precious a commodity time is in our classrooms. Of course, what we learn about our students and their needs and interests will require us to revisit and adjust the plans we make at this point, but our plans can still guide our overall work across the year. Planning across the year also helps us to avoid both moving too slowly and attempting to cram too many things in at once: when we know that we have a schedule to keep, we can keep it at a reasonable pace. This prevents students from getting bored and from feeling overwhelmed.

Part of the evaluation system looks at planning, and your ability to articulate why you chose specific activities or sequenced lessons in a certain order is essential for demonstrating your planning ability. Stepping back and doing a big-picture glance at the year helps you think about the overall decisions. Are there particular concepts that are tricky or that students struggle with? Perhaps you come back to those concepts in another unit to reinforce and to reteach them in a different context. Maybe you create stations to allow students to explore the concepts in different ways or look at both examples and nonexamples to clarify their thinking. Taking time at the start to think through how much time you have overall will help you help students learn more and more deeply, and, evaluations aside, that is our ultimate goal as educators.

If you aren't already in the habit of planning units for the entire year ahead of time, making this plan may look like a daunting task. Your goal is to chunk out skills and content that need to be introduced, refined, or mastered in each unit and to have an idea of what the lesson plans will encompass. However, now is not the time to write detailed lesson plans for each day—you'll write the specifics of your daily lesson plans as the year unfolds, with this progression and your own students in mind. As middle school English language arts and history teacher Keisha Rembert explains, "don't start with last year's lesson plans; . . . start with the kids [you] have in front of [you], and then . . . go back to resources from last year."

Planning Lessons

As you write lessons during the year, you do not have to reinvent the wheel each day. In fact, it might be better for your students if you don't. Using lesson frames or templates balances direct instruction with time for students to apply what they've learned and teacher-focused time with student-focused time. If your classroom is run as a workshop, you're likely already using a basic template for your lesson planning, perhaps a short lesson followed by time for students to work, with you conferring with students as necessary. For math, you might have a benchmark lesson—a demonstration about how to use manipulatives or create a diagram, for example—followed by student problem solving. Science teachers use this format often, with a lab demonstration followed by lab procedures and lab reports. In these models, students understand that what they are learning always has an application. While allowing for flexibility to include other work, this template lets students use the predictable nature of the class to form their own routines and strategies, to reflect on their learning, and to stay on task and productive.

Using lesson frames does not mean that every day is identical. English teacher and author Penny Kittle notes that the daily schedule in her block English class, "like all lesson plans, . . . is subject to variation, interruption, and teachable moments. What is predictable is time to read and write in a supportive, structured environment to improve" (2008, 70). Teaching requires a balance of routine (so class flows smoothly) and innovation (to keep students interested and to help with retention). In literature class, perhaps the lesson frame is a close reading exercise followed by small-group discussions of the close reading. This leaves flexibility regarding the exercise (What is the reading passage? What is the lens?), the discussion (Are they expert groups that then report out? Jigsaws? Mixed groups?), and the product of the groups' work (A list of imagery? A response that uses the key words from the passage? Written group responses to other groups' work?). In this way, what students read or how they respond can vary, but the expectation that they will work as individuals and then in small groups where they will create something to share will stay the same. The Danielson evaluation model values using routines where students are driving the activity in the classroom, but it also values innovation and creativity in lesson planning. In addition, it values changing grouping patterns. Aim to strike a balance so that the disruptions to the routine seem more like brain breaks or mini-vacations rather than a lack of routine altogether.

Coplanning

For those of us who coteach, coplanning often presents its own challenges. Before you begin the year, have a frank discussion about how comfortable you each are with the content. Don't assume a certificate completely defines what your coteacher knows and can do in a classroom. I have a degree in American studies, for example, but my colleagues typically don't know that unless they teach or plan with me.

In my own coteaching work, my coteacher and I used weekly calendar pages (see Professional Journal Page 4.02) to map out what needed to be done each week and which pieces of the unit plan would be taught when. We planned from the end of the unit backward so that the instruction was organized in a way that made sense for student learning and still gave us time for reteaching or spillover if interruptions prevented our plan from staying on track (such as the day all of the students were called out of class for vision screenings). We also kept the plans for future weeks handy so we could jot down any lessons that needed to be added, retaught, or rescheduled while we were in class and it was fresh in our minds. The weekly plan notes made writing up individual lesson plans later much easier because we had a road map for each unit from the beginning of the year.

On our plans, we noted the following:

- what we knew students typically struggled with

- sections that we could chunk or compact if need be

- the skills or accommodations called for in the basic skills curriculum or students' plans that we were incorporating

- who was teaching which part of the lesson each day

- who was handling preparation of different materials (to avoid the "I thought you were writing the quiz" confusion that sometimes comes in the rush to squeeze everything in)

Keep Students First

By planning the curriculum at the unit level and weaving through the content, student skills, expectations, and curricular requirements with the demands of the evaluation rubric before beginning, we can take pressure off ourselves to do things for the sake of doing them and keep the focus on what students need to know and to be able to do. Planning the curriculum to match up with how we are being evaluated means that we are not asking students to put on a performance for the observer. Instead, the observer gets to see the choices we have made deliberately to showcase our best practice and most accomplished teaching by putting our children's needs first from the beginning, giving them time to learn routines and focus on skills and content in each unit. While it makes more work for us up front, it takes pressure off us throughout the school year because we have a plan and have given some thought to each unit already.

See Professional Journal Page 4.02 at the end of this chapter for a reproducible chart to help you plan.

(Also available online as a digital download.)

We are never facing a blank planning sheet with no idea where to begin. The planning calendar gives us a place to jot down how lessons went and to make notes for future units right in the preliminary plans for those units. Instead of a sticky note that I might not find when I am writing a unit plan six months later, I have a note to myself in the planning calendar to group students differently for a similar project, or to try something new, or to revise the directions of a task. I don't need to shuffle binders of work and try to find where to put the note—the planning calendar has all the curriculum notes where I need them. This again lets me think about how my students respond to the curriculum rather than rely on planning in a vacuum without them. Because once we know our students, we can begin making our lessons more relevant.

Planning the Year: A Checklist

This is a quick guide to mapping out your year and your units, whether you're working with hard copies of yearly and monthly calendars or with a digital calendar.

The Big Picture (for Your Year-at-a-Glance Calendar)

Mark the following days:

- ☐ beginning and end of the year
- ☐ holidays
- ☐ school closings
- ☐ standardized testing days
- ☐ exam days
- ☐ ends of marking periods
- ☐ dates when grades are due (also mark the next day as a time to reflect)
- ☐ dates when progress reports are due (also mark the next day as a time to reflect)
- ☐ school-wide events
- ☐ any other interruptions in the schedule that are already planned

As you look at the chunks of time that remain, sketch out where your units will fit. A few suggestions:

- Reserve some time early in the year for getting to know students and establishing routines.
- Use periods of uninterrupted time for your meatiest units.
- Give yourself a few days between units to give students more time with a concept if it proves necessary or to make up lost time.

Month-by-Month Details (for Your Monthly Calendars)

If you're working on paper, transfer your notes from your yearly calendar to your monthly calendars. Then add the following plans.

At the beginning of the year:

- ☐ Mark days for getting to know students and establishing routines.

Within each unit:

- ☐ List the skills you want students to focus on in the unit.
- ☐ List strategies, lessons, and activities you plan to use in the unit (being mindful of the parts of the lessons that evaluation models require *and* of the work that demonstrates your best teaching).

Daily Lesson Planning

Think about the following questions:

What elements might be helpful to include in a daily lesson frame?

How will these daily elements help students?

Class: _____   Week's Focus: _____

Monday   **Date:**

Notes

Teacher: Teacher:

Preparation

Delivery

Tuesday   **Date:**

Notes

Teacher: Teacher:

Preparation

Delivery

continues   **67**

4.02   **Coplanning Guide** *continued*

Wednesday   **Date:**

Notes

| Teacher: | Teacher: |

Preparation

Delivery

Thursday   **Date:**

Notes

| Teacher: | Teacher: |

Preparation

Delivery

Friday   **Date:**

Notes

| Teacher: | Teacher: |

Preparation

Delivery

Learning More About Your Students

As a new teacher, I thought I got to know my students fairly well. I talked with them at the door about their day or what was happening in their lives. We made connections, but what I learned was haphazard.

I learned just how much I was missing when I was grading some student writing. Juan, one of my juniors, was consistently making verb-tense errors. This might have led me to believe that Juan needed help with verb tense. Yet, when I thought about instances when I'd heard Juan speak, I didn't recall hearing those errors. The next day, when I showed Juan the issue I'd spotted in his writing, Juan examined the paper and shook his head. "I know that's wrong. I can't believe I did that." We talked a bit. I learned that at home, Juan spoke both English and Spanish with his parents. We realized that when Juan was doing his writing at home—hurriedly, he admitted, and often while talking with his family—he might have been shifting into using tenses that were more consistent with Spanish than with English.

Bringing the issue to Juan's attention was all it took to fix it. It saved both of us a lot of long explanations and practice that was unnecessary because he knew the rule but he just wasn't applying it in a certain case.

From then on, I made sure to ask students what languages were spoken in the home. Thinking about it more, I started to wonder if there was other information I should be gathering from students more consistently and if I was missing out on opportunities to connect and to help my students learn. As my colleague Luann Christensen Lee once said, "there's always a 'why' to kid behavior; it's up to us to use that."

Many current evaluation models focus on how teachers make decisions, but the key to every teacher decision should always be the students. While the most important piece of this work is obviously the benefit it has for our students, getting to know our students also makes us more able to meet the requirements of our evaluations and to explain our instructional decisions to observers and administrators. In addition, most evaluation models expect teachers to have knowledge of their students' backgrounds, interests, and needs as a specific area of the evaluation. We can share with evaluators artifacts that include information sheets, inventories, samples of work where students could explore their own interests, and anecdotal notes about conversations with students in pre- and postconferences as evidence that we know our students and are thinking systematically about how to use that information to teach them.

Once we have a plan for the year's journey, we can adjust it based on our students' needs. The more information we gather from a variety of sources, the more quickly we can adjust and the better we can explain our instructional decisions. I keep a binder of student information separated by class and then by student. Not only does it help me show how I'm specifically gathering student information from a variety of sources, as the evaluation model articulates, but it makes it easier to plan or discuss issues with parents or other school personnel because I have all the information in one place. I keep my specific notes about conversations with parents in this binder, where my parent contact log just lists the date, the student, the mode of communication (email, phone, note home, etc.), and the overall topic discussed, such as homework or behavior. In one glance, an administrator can see the modes and frequency of parent communication on the log, and at the same time, I have more detailed student notes and information in a central location.

Consider a time you connected with a student personally and it helped you reach that child in the classroom academically. How did you make that connection? How did you apply it? By reflecting on how you've been successful in connecting with students, you can be systematic in how you collect the information you need. In this chapter, I address ways to use what you've learned to connect with your students in order to make the content meaningful for them and to tailor your yearlong plans for them.

Get to Know Your New Students

If you are getting all new students, the following ideas from Donald Graves (2001) are excellent ways to check your progress in learning about your students. If you know some of your students already or have already met your classes, Graves offered a way to think about what you know about your students, and which students you know. First, make a three-column chart. Then, from memory, list each student's name in the first column. In the second column, list experiences, skills, or interests of each child, and in the final column, check off a student when you confirm that the child knows you know these things about him or her. When you finish, check the list against your roster to see which students you forgot and consider why you know more about certain students (25). After this process, Graves set about getting to know the students he forgot better. He made a point of observing the students outside of his own classroom, taking time to watch them for a few minutes in art or physical education. He explained, "I want to move away from the more dominant way of knowing children through spoken words and written words, and catch other abilities and impressions. I also find it useful to try to look at the world through their eyes. I try to become that child" (29). We've all known students who were engaged and willing participants in our classes but seemed to struggle in others. This method of rounding out our view of students may help us find more connections we can make to help students feel safe and valued in our classrooms, in turn increasing their achievement.

Get Curious About Your Students

A colleague of mine once said that she didn't think to collect information about students because she didn't think it applied to her as a math teacher. In truth, we never know what bit of information will help us to forge a connection with students or to see things from their point of view. I often think of fellow teacher Luann Christensen Lee, who learns what careers her students are interested in and then explains how her subject, chemistry, will help them as beauticians, reporters, and veterinarians. What moments of insight have you shared with a student because of a connection?

Learn About Your Students' Lives in School

There's no single list of useful topics when getting to know your students. They are, after all, multifaceted human beings who can't be put into categories any more accurately than we ourselves can. However, there are some topics that seem to be easy starting places in a school setting. For example, you can have a quick chat as students are coming into the classroom about **school activities and sports** they participate in. Showing students you know them as people outside the classroom often goes a long way toward convincing them you care and want them to learn. When you need more information about a student, knowing which advisors or coaches to approach to give more insight about that student helps, too.

Listening with care when students discuss **pop culture, sports, entertainment, and media** may help you to see what they value and, at the very least, will give you an idea of what pop-culture references will resonate with them.

You can quickly take the temperature of a new class by asking students about **past experiences in their subject area**, how they learn best, a favorite project they did in the past and why, and what they hope to learn in your class.

Learn About Your Students' Lives Beyond School

Knowing your students also means you know what responsibilities or obstacles they have outside school. "I ask if they have Internet access at home, a printer, a computer, a cell phone," special education history teacher Lisa Sidorick-Weise explains. "I ask who needs to get younger siblings off the bus or is responsible for siblings when they get home. This way I know what needs to be done in school and what they can realistically finish at home."

Because students might feel pressure to answer the questions teachers ask, we must be careful about what we ask them. They might not feel that they can politely refuse our requests, which could cause stress, embarrassment, and anger. It's best to avoid questions that could expose sensitive issues. Beware of focusing questions tightly on a particular topic that might make them feel cornered; for example, "What's your favorite app?" might make them feel that they have to share that they can't afford a smartphone or tablet. Instead, try leading with broader questions, like "What do you like to do in your free time?" Or, better yet, try listening to the topics they bring up on their own.

While we would like to believe all of our students come from supportive, healthy families, sometimes when we listen, we discover that this is not the case. Knowing our students helps us create safer places for them to learn. It also helps us to know when and how to bring in other school resources for support when needed. In an article about student trauma and its implications, psychiatrist Bruce D. Perry warns, "Even without overt experiences of trauma, children who live in stressful environments of poverty don't internalize new information at the same rate as children who enter the classroom in a calm state. Year after year, traumatized students learn at a slower rate, disengage, and ultimately fall behind—a vicious cycle that all too often leads them to drop out of school" (2016).

As a good rule of thumb, being curious about our students rather than being judgmental will help us to learn about them quickly. This means that when they insult our favorite team, for example, our response should not be to take offense, but to ask them *why* they feel that way. It might be that they come from a long line of fans of a rival team. Or it might be that they don't know as much about our team as we do. Or it might just mean that they're looking for someone to engage with them about their opinions.

Collect Information in a Variety of Ways

While one of the best ways to collect information is to ask for it at the start of the year, you can make the process of getting to know your students something that happens all year long. Here are a few suggestions.

Start the Year with Student Information Sheets

On the first day of class, I find students are open and will answer most questions without concern that it will lead to an assignment (my students often become cagier as the year goes on). I start the year with an information sheet (see Professional Journal Page 5.01), returning the original to them and putting a photocopy in the separate binder I keep for student information so I can refer to it quickly throughout the year. I also put a few representative examples, with names removed for confidentiality, in my professional development journal. These artifacts help to demonstrate my knowledge of students.

The questions on this sheet are simple; I ask whom they live with (you don't have to be in teaching long to discover how easy it is to offend someone by referring to an aunt as a parent, and the fields on the school records are not always clear or updated), their address, and a phone number for sharing good news with their grown-ups (I follow through on that and try to call parents and guardians to introduce myself during the first couple weeks of school). I ask about how they spend their time and about television they watch, YouTube creators they follow, and social media accounts they keep up with. I often change the questions depending on the class I'm teaching. Some years I offer "would you rather" scenarios, and other years I ask a few multiple-choice questions to mix it up, depending on how much class time we have on the first day. I explain to students that I will not be sharing this information with the class—it's just to help me get to know them and to help me know what kinds of help they might need. Students who don't have Internet access, for example, might

5.01

See Professional Journal Page 5.01 at the end of this chapter for a reproducible questionnaire to use with students.

(Also available online as a digital download.)

need more flexibility in turning in online assignments. I also let them know that they don't need to answer any questions they'd rather not answer.

Over the first week or two of school, I collect more information, spreading out my requests so as not to overwhelm students. (This is where that time that I built into the first days of class on my calendar comes in handy—it gives me a cushion of time so that I don't feel that I need to rush through this process.) I ask students to share more about themselves in writing, letting them know that these pieces will be shared with the class. Asking where students have lived, what they're most proud of, something they want to do someday, or something they've never done, or offering prompts about favorite movies, genres, actors, and such tends to get students sharing about themselves. The students' responses are always interesting, but watching them complete these assignments tells me a lot about personalities, work habits, and interests right away. I can see which students I should put together if I want to make a design-expert group (or whom to separate if I want each group to have someone who can draw and design well). I know who rushes to complete the assignment, even leaving some areas blank, and who works methodically. Which ones can't finish even when I give updates on how much time is remaining? Hanging these pieces up and letting students discuss the results is one of our first bonding moments. Other ideas include icebreaker bingo games and scavenger hunts to let students work together and separately to see who leads and who follows. As a result, I start the year with some insight into personalities and talents, both demonstrated and bragged about (the disconnects between the kids who insist they "can't draw" and then make pretty good doodles of their pets are telling).

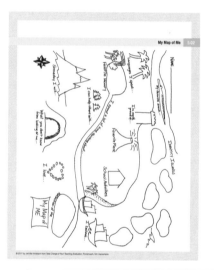

See Professional Journal Page 5.02 at the end of this chapter for a reproducible sheet to use with students.

(Also available online as a digital download.)

Use Student Inventories

As an English teacher, I ask students to take inventories, or questionnaires, on their lives as readers and writers. They usually complete these one at a time over several days—they are great bell-work activities. Students write their reading autobiographies and writing autobiographies, which tell the story of their literacy lives. For example, in a reading autobiography, a student might tell about her memories of being read to before she could read, of the pride she took in her early days of reading, of her favorite childhood books, and of the place reading has in her life now. All of this gives me insight into how they feel about my content area and the value they place on it. I use these to customize learning, to get insight into how to approach them, and to gauge progress over the year. One of my favorite moments was at the end of the year when a student observed that his reading inventory from the beginning of the year made it look "like it was illegal" in his house to be caught with a book; that young man had blossomed into a voracious reader over the course of the year.

Figure 5.1a–b After a lesson on self-identity, students create these maps about themselves to be posted in the classroom.

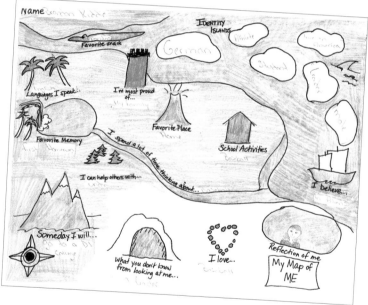

Asking students about what they want to do when they leave high school and what they see themselves doing in ten and twenty-five years also gives me insight into what they need from my class. High school juniors who say they hate reading but declare they are going to medical school might be persuaded to build reading stamina and writing skills if I can show them what they'll need to get through medical school. While this example is obviously closely tied to one discipline, you can create an inventory for your own content area, as well—how are your students as scientists, mathematicians, historians, linguists, engineers, musicians, or artists?

Reach Out to Families

Another way I collect information that gives me insight into a student is to ask parents or guardians to tell me what their child's strengths and areas for growth are, what the child wants to do outside high school, and what career path the child is considering. These are great questions for a back-to-school night, but they might also come up during other conversations. The contradictions in what family members report and what your students tell you are often informative. I always ask parents and guardians what they want me to know about their children. Brace yourself: this question is powerful. When I've asked it, I've learned about cancer that students wouldn't speak about, foster homes, and families who had moved many times or who had recently lost a parent. While students are in my class, I need to build a relationship with their families, and asking parents and guardians about their children is one of the best ways to show that I care.

Open Up an Ongoing Dialogue with Students

There are many ways to involve students in dialogue. Because I teach high school, I have a lot of students every day and worry about overlooking a student. Responding to their writing journals, where they often write about what they are thinking about, is one way I keep in touch. I also use book letters, adapted from Donalyn Miller's *Book Whisperer* (2009), which gives me a way to respond to students and have a conversation through their letters twice a month. Students write about what they are reading and are free to write to me about anything else they want to share. However, there are many other strategies.

See Professional Journal Pages 5.03 and 5.04 at the end of this chapter for a reproducible parent/guardian information sheet and a reproducible contact information log for your professional development journal.

(Also available online as a digital download.)

One strategy is using a "weekly calendar page," as described by literacy author and high school reading specialist Cris Tovani (2000; 2011). Each week, she gives students a page with five large boxes and asks them to use a box each day to write to her, leaving space for her to respond. She then writes back to each student. She explains that using "conversation calendars" gives her insight into her students' lives and interests and helps her personalize their learning.

Use What You've Learned About Your Students

The first and most obvious way to put what you've learned about your students to use is to build strong relationships with them. "You can't have my mind if you don't have my heart," middle school English language arts and history teacher Keisha Rembert said of why she works hard to learn about her students. "When you are with students for one hundred minutes a day, there needs to be a comfort level."

What you learn about your students is also an important factor in your academic work with students across the year. Consider the following ways in which you can tailor your work to your students' needs.

Consider Students' Resources as You Plan

Keep students' resources in mind as you design curriculum. For example, if students don't have Internet access at home, asking them to do online research on their own each night might cause difficulties. You might also ask students who have some experience or expertise that relates to what you are studying to share what they know.

Make Your Work in the Classroom More Relevant to Their Lives

"If I have a student who wants to be a chemical engineer, when I form groups I can make sure I have one student who wants to pursue chemistry in each group, or I can put them all in one group, where like minds can problem solve," Luann Christensen Lee explains. Knowing her students allows Luann to change the way she designs assignments so that students feel empowered.

Give Students the Opportunity to Focus on What Is Important to Them

Over the past several years, I've been fortunate to work with three outstanding English teachers in other schools—Lee Ann Spillane, Sarah Mulhern Gross, and Christine Kervina—to help our students engage in real-world argument writing by creating videos for charities to raise both awareness and money through the Project for Awesome. The charities that the students support are often related to causes that students hold dear. For example, in my class, after a student shared how she lost her mother a few years ago, she also shared that a local grief center for children helped her. Two other students immediately stepped up when it came time to select charities and helped her create a video that was important to her.

Figure 5.2 Making space in the classroom to honor students' identities, families, and culture helps to make the classroom their space.

Give Students Opportunities to Involve Their Families and Culture

Try to weave in activities that involve your students' families and culture throughout the year. When I teach the American dream, I ask students to learn about what the American dream means to their parents or grandparents and to write about how their own dreams are similar or different. My film students watch one of their older family member's favorite films with them and then discuss the experience with the class. Students are honoring how their identity shapes their understanding of the world around them.

Make Your Students Part of Your Yearlong Plan

Now that you've considered different ways to make students' perspectives, needs, and backgrounds a part of your class, make plans for putting these considerations into action. Take a moment to revisit your notes on your action plan for the year (Professional Journal Page 3.02) and on the monthly calendars you laid out (see Chapter 4). What topics or pedagogy do you want to learn more about as a result of what you've learned about your students? Note these ideas on your action plan, and begin the process of looking into sources you might learn from. What aspects of what you've learned about your students might affect the plans you mapped out for the year? Add notes to your calendar to remind yourself of how you might connect upcoming lessons to your students' experiences and needs. Finally, make copies of the student artifacts that have given you the most helpful insights and add them to your journal. This should be a representative sample, not everything you collected and used. These may be the student information pages from this chapter or any other documentation that has given you valuable information about your students. Use Professional Journal Page 5.05 to organize the artifacts you include.

See Professional Journal Page 5.05 at the end of this chapter for a reproducible log.

(Also available online as a digital download.)

Keep Students First

Using the information we gather from and about students centers our teaching practice upon them, their interests, and their needs. By incorporating our students' backgrounds into our teaching, we can make students feel invested in the process, in the product, or in the people in our classrooms, all of which contribute to increased learning. The ethic of caring, required by our profession, also means that we can see shifts in students and identify those who may need more support or interventions, keeping our students safe and healthy. Giving students ownership of what they study or how they learn it shows them that they are valued members of our classrooms.

Name: _____ Date: _____ Class: _____

What do you prefer to be called? _____

Whom do you live with? _____

_____

What's the best number to reach your parent/guardian to tell him or her how you're doing? _____

_____

What is your mailing address? _____

_____

What languages are spoken in your home? _____

_____

How do you spend your time outside school? _____

_____

What activities/sports/hobbies do you participate in? _____

_____

What's the last book you read? _____

What was the last *good* book you read? What did you like about it? _____

_____

In school, you're best at _____ .

In school, you struggle with _____ .

How much time do you spend on homework each night? _____

Where have you lived? _____

_____

If you could go anywhere, where would you go? Why? _____

_____

Do you play videogames? If so, what titles are your favorites? _____

_____

What wouldn't I know about you just from looking at you? _____

_____

How do you learn best? How do you know? _____

_____

What are you favorite movies? TV shows? YouTubers/channels? _____

_____

Do you have a computer at home?	☐ Yes	☐ Usually	☐ Not often	☐ No
Do you have Internet access at home?	☐ Yes	☐ Usually	☐ Not often	☐ No
Do you have a printer at home?	☐ Yes	☐ Usually	☐ Not often	☐ No
Do you have a cell phone with Internet access?	☐ Yes	☐ Usually	☐ Not often	☐ No
Do you have a cell phone with texting?	☐ Yes	☐ Usually	☐ Not often	☐ No
Do you have message limits on your texts?	☐ Yes	☐ Usually	☐ Not often	☐ No

What do you want me to know about you? _____

_____

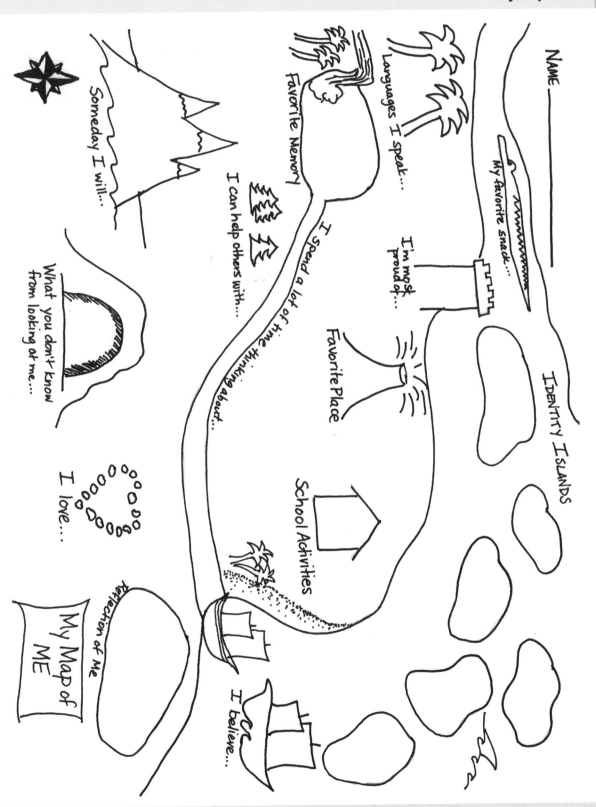

NAME _____

My favorite snack...

IDENTITY ISLANDS

Languages I speak...

Favorite Memory

Someday I will...

I can help others with...

I spend a lot of time thinking about...

I'm most proud of...

Favorite Place

What you don't know from looking at me...

School Activities

I love...

Reflection of Me

My Map of ME

I believe...

81

Dear Parents/Guardians:

This year, your child will be in my class. To help me get to know your child, please complete this information sheet and return it with your child. I'm looking forward to working with you this year to help your child succeed. Thank you!

How would you describe your child?

_____
_____
_____
_____

What are your child's strengths?

_____
_____
_____
_____

In what areas does your child struggle in school?

_____
_____
_____

How does your child learn best?

_____
_____
_____
_____

What are your child's plans for the future?

_____
_____
_____

What should I know about your child to be able to help him or her learn best this year?

_____
_____
_____

What phone number is best to reach you during the school day?

_____

What email address can I use to send you updates on your child's progress?

_____

What else do you want me to know about your child?

_____
_____
_____
_____

Student: _____

Date	Mode of Communication	Family Member	Notes (Consider: What, if anything, did I learn about this student from this exchange?)

Student	Date	Artifact	How I Plan to Use What I Learned from This Artifact

Preparing for Your Announced Observation

Recently I was talking to a colleague about her evaluation. She was discouraged. She felt the evaluation did not reflect her planning and her knowledge of her students and content. She felt as though the evaluator hadn't seen the full picture of her work.

"Did you put all that information in your preconference forms?" I asked.

"No. I didn't want to say too much because then they could hold me accountable for what I said."

Wait. In the high-stakes world of evaluations, it might seem like a smart move to not tip your hand in the preconference documents (the documentation that you prepare for your meeting with your observer before the observation). But, when we don't show our evaluators what we are doing in our classrooms, we don't give them the opportunity to understand our process and, in turn, to give us credit for that process. As teachers, our work is about doing the best we can for each student. We need to show evaluators that work.

The preconference is your chance to show what you know about your content, your students, and your pedagogy.

Filling out preconference paperwork is a requirement for most evaluation systems. However, preparing for the observation can be much more productive for your practice, for your students, and for your career if you view this work as a personal status check on how you are doing. This chapter focuses on setting aside time to reflect on your practice and your goals, consider how you can continue to grow, focus on what you want the observer to see in your work, and present your work so that the observer can see how you are helping your students.

Put the Observation Forms Aside and Reflect on Your Work So Far

The preconference forms that you are required to complete have their own built-in perspectives. For now, let's set those forms aside and focus on you: your goals, your practice, and your growth.

When someone comes into your classroom, they are there for only a snippet of the ongoing story of your classroom. Your job is to provide them with a context for interpreting what is happening. This will help them to understand how the work you're doing is helping students. It will show how clearly you know your students' needs and how you have tailored the class to address those needs.

Reflect first on the lessons you have been teaching so far. What has gone well? How do you know? What evidence can you point to? Is the class ahead or behind of where you thought you would be when you made your original plan for the year? Why? Consider what activities you have planned and experiences you have structured. How did your students respond? Where are the strengths as a class? Where do you need to help them grow? Keep your students in mind on observation day just as you would on any day: if they are likely to struggle unproductively with the activity you have planned, plan a different activity or change your approach to the original activity.

And while you are reflecting on the lessons and the learning, take a moment to think about the routines you set up in the beginning of the year. How efficient are they? Are students remembering on their own, or do you need to post more signage or rearrange supplies for the routine to be more intuitive? If your routines are efficient and working, take a moment to reflect on how you designed them to be that way. What did you take into account?

Now go back to the personal-growth plan you made for yourself for the year (see Professional Journal Page 2.03). Think about where you are and where you hoped you would be at this point. Do you need to go back and do some research to be prepared? Have you addressed any perceived weaknesses from last year's evaluations? Make sure you have concrete evidence of what you have done to strengthen your practice.

6.01

See Professional Journal Page 6.01 at the end of this chapter for a note-taking guide for your preconference documentation.

(Also available online as a digital download.)

Consider Your Classes' Progress

Now, think about what is currently going on in your classroom. Make a quick list of what you can point to that students have learned so far this year. What products do you have that show this? Consider whether they have mastered the material you are referring to or if they are making progress in the journey. Think about what students have learned beyond content knowledge: Are they better at discussion? Can they speak to each other instead of looking for you to moderate every comment? Have they grown in how they participate in groups? All of this information will be important when you discuss what you are teaching next and why.

Double-check that you can discuss the goals of both the unit and the lesson. What will students be able to do? If you teach with essential questions and guiding questions, make sure they are in alignment and make sense in terms of larger assessments, such as the midterm and final exams. Consider what comes next in your unit, too. What skills and content are you teaching now that they will use later? How have you structured the unit to help students make sense of ideas? Be prepared to explain which parts of the lesson or unit come from your own new learning or how you modified them based on student performance, peer feedback, or your own reflection.

You can also help the observer to understand your students' unique needs. Documenting each child either with initials or without using a name ("one child has lost a family member recently" or "two children have IEPs that require the following accommodations," for example) demonstrates that you know your students, and it allows you to show that you are adjusting your instruction for them. Likewise, if a student doesn't participate the way a reviewer might expect, your previous documentation of issues will show the observer that you are already aware of your students' needs. You can then discuss the issue with the observer in the postobservation conversation without being worried that he or she will consider this background information to be merely excuses about something that happened in class.

6.02

See Professional Journal Page 6.02 at the end of this chapter for a note-taking guide for your preconference documentation.

(Also available online as a digital download.)

Helping Students Make Sense of Ideas

It is not vital that information be predigested for students. Research (Zwiers and Crawford 2011) shows that we might be overscaffolding for students (165). In our hurry to show how accomplished we are at breaking down tasks, we have eliminated letting students wrestle with problems, pointing the way to clearly defined solutions. Instead, be certain that you can show how you have provided students resources to help them with the struggle, such as benchmark lessons, information about similar problems that they could apply to the current one, diagrams, or instruction in skills such as close reading or evaluating arguments.

Consider Where You Can Grow

Sometimes we are hesitant to name how we want to improve. It might feel like we're admitting that we aren't currently good enough or are deficient in some way. However, I don't believe in that deficit mind-set. When a surgeon creates a new technique, it doesn't mean she wasn't proficient at her job before that. Saying you have an area for growth is not the same as saying you are completely deficient at something. It's smart to build on our strengths, to expand our repertoire of skills, and to deepen our knowledge and understanding of concepts.

When you go into your preconference, how you approach it may depend upon your comfort level and relationship with your observer. If your area of concern is one that your observer is already aware of, document your attempts to grow in that area and to apply that knowledge in your classroom. If it's an area that you worry may not go well during the lesson, especially if it's an ongoing issue, address it head-on by saying, "I've been working in this area recently to strengthen my practice." Provide your documentation and any evidence or data you have gathered. If your observer is someone you trust, ask for genuine feedback on what steps he or she thinks you should take next to keep growing. Frame everything as an opportunity to grow, just as you would for a student. And don't forget that even master teachers struggle when attempting something new (Fullan 1993). Keep smiling and showcase your efforts and your students' efforts in the best possible light.

Plan Your Observation Lesson

Once you know when you will be observed, your topic of instruction will likely be narrowed to what you had intended for that day. As you decide on a lesson, consider your strengths and areas you want to demonstrate as well as the evaluation rubrics that are used for announced observations.

If you know you need a strong lesson because your teaching has not been scored as high as you believe it should have been or if you are working to show improvement, choose a lesson format that students find engaging and have demonstrated success in.

In this case, it is not time to break out something totally new but to show that your students are growing and connecting meaningfully with the content while demonstrating the skills you are assessing. Prepare your observer during the preconference by offering the evidence you've used to make your decisions and mentioning other ideas and strategies you've tried or considered (and why you aren't using them here), and let the observer know what criteria you are using to determine student growth or proficiency. If you have a coaching relationship with your observer or the style is more collegial, don't hesitate to say, "I'm proud of the work I've done on X and look forward to your feedback on improving Y." Make sure that you have planned a lesson with strengths you can point to instead of leaving things up to chance.

Once you have planned your lesson, prepare a second activity as a backup in case there is a major disruption. I've had observed lessons when half the class was on a field trip, so we couldn't do our group activity. Choose something that aligns with your original goals for the lesson but can be done independently or in small groups. The backup activity should be something your students know procedures for and are familiar with. Have copies of extra background information or notes for students who may have been absent for an extended period of time (or a new student who transfers in the day of your observation, which has happened to me—it's always good to have a new-student "Welcome to Our Class" kit waiting to go).

As a final check on your lesson plan, you could peek ahead at Professional Journal Page 8.02, which is designed to help you assess how the observed lesson went. It can also be a helpful tool in considering how this lesson is a good fit for the students in your class.

Draft Your Preconference Documentation and Include Artifacts

When you sit down to fill in the preobservation forms your school requires, set aside plenty of time. Using your notes in your professional development journal, look for places in the forms where you can tell the observer about your strengths (Journal Pages 2.01, 2.02, and 2.03) and about how your work is helping your students (Journal Pages 6.01 and 6.02). Answer each question as thoroughly as you can. For example, in the Danielson model, knowledge of students requires teachers to collect information about students systematically using multiple sources of information. Document both that you have information about individual students and that it is from multiple sources. Emphasize where you are reflective and where you make adjustments for student needs.

What Evidence Might You Include in the Pre-Conference Documentation?

Pertinent artifacts are evidence that your teaching is highly effective and you are engaged with the students and their learning.

To give you an overview, I've included my preconference artifacts for a recent observation of my students engaging in an end-of-unit Socratic seminar. My preconference forms explained each of these items in more detail.

Instructional Materials I Planned to Use During the Lesson

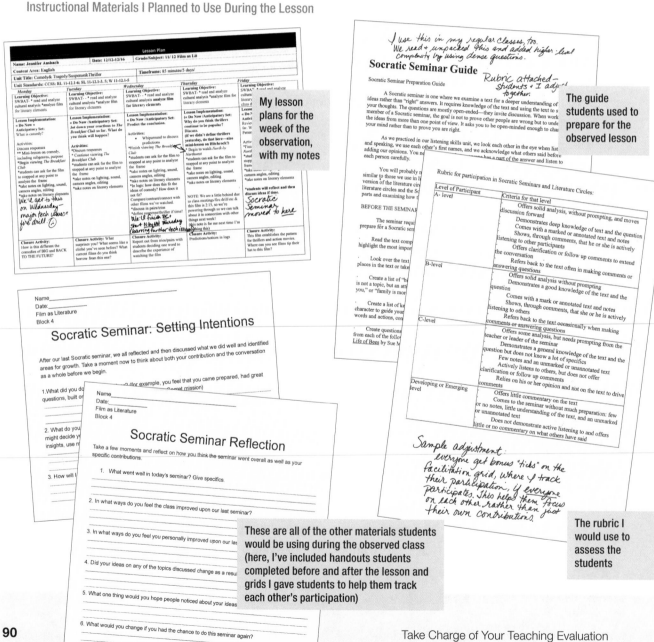

My lesson plans for the week of the observation, with my notes

The guide students used to prepare for the observed lesson

The rubric I would use to assess the students

These are all of the other materials students would be using during the observed class (here, I've included handouts students completed before and after the lesson and grids I gave students to help them track each other's participation)

Artifacts to Support What I Did and Why

Don't worry that you might be including too many artifacts—as long as there's a purpose for each item you're including, you can trust that the observer will decide what he or she wants to read and what to simply skim. Including these artifacts also gives the evaluator something to refer to as he or she considers what he or she observed in your class.

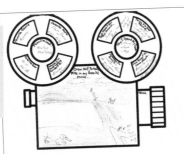

Copies of student writing about themselves from the first week of school to help the observer see that I was actively working to get to know my students

Lesson plans for the week prior to the observation, annotated with reflections and notes on how the lessons were connected to prior learning

Previous student work samples and reflections that showed that the work we were doing in this class was connected to the skills we had been working on over time

Facilitation grid from previous seminar to show how this class had done this type of assignment in the past

Materials that would help the observer see how this lesson was part of ongoing work and the resources I had provided students (here, I've included a printout of the website I maintain for students and pages of instructional handouts that students had used so the observer could see what students were using)

Use the Evaluation Rubric to Fine-Tune Your Documentation

A teacher I know, Luann, aligns all of her plans to her evaluation rubric. She explains that because she thinks reflectively as a habit, explaining how her decisions align with her instructional goals, where students are, and where students are going isn't difficult. Another colleague, Lisa, explains, "When I make my lesson plan, I'm not thinking about the evaluation rubric—I'm thinking about the curriculum." Over the years, she has created a library of resources of varying strategies so she can meet individual needs, and she's reflective about planning her lessons, making sure that the students have a good variety in their assignments. Then, when she prepares for an observation, she looks at the evaluation rubric to see how her work meets the requirements.

Whether your approach is more like Luann's, more like Lisa's, or somewhere in between, it's a good idea to set aside time to go through each section of the form you've completed, this time with the evaluation rubric and your analysis of the rubric from Chapter 3 (Professional Journal Page 3.01). Wherever possible, align your language in your preconference document to the language of the rubric. Just as you did when you analyzed the rubric earlier, focus on the highest level of achievement on the rubric, not the level that merely shows compliance. Using the language of the scoring rubric makes it easier to demonstrate the connection between what you are producing and the levels of performance expected. More than once I have become flustered in a meeting and was thankful when the language was an exact match so I could point out the alignment of my work with the performance rubric.

Be thorough and scrutinize each section. If you need to add something to your lesson plan to earn the top score, do that now. This kind of highly detailed planning may feel odd at first—on most days, if you forget to point out a connection to something, you always have tomorrow. But this is not most days; it's one of only a few opportunities to show your work to an observer. The planning portion of the rubric is the one you get to prepare ahead of time; scoring high on this section may be labor-intensive, but it is not out of reach.

Finally, consider what you need to include to help your observer understand your lesson. Prepare your preconference documentation and artifacts to support your observer in following your lesson, especially if your content is specialized, such as a world language, ceramics, computer design and drafting, or calculus. For example, Spanish teacher Aracelli Iacovelli explains that when she's putting together her preconference documents, she needs to be detailed about her vocabulary and the structure of her lesson because her observers don't speak Spanish, the language in which she teaches the majority of her classes.

Use the Conference to Give Evidence of Your Strong Work

Most evaluation models and districts use a protocol for the preconference itself. In many cases, you submit your answers to preconference questions ahead of time, and then the conversation delves into those answers. If you prepared your responses thoroughly and put together an array of artifacts that address the range of evaluation criteria covered in preconferences, you should be completely prepared to offer not only your insights but your evidence to back up how you have determined your next steps.

But what if there isn't a protocol or clear agenda? While this is not usually the case, make sure you offer ideas for what you'll be doing in the lesson and, more important, why you're doing it. Provide your evidence for your decisions and the goals you have for students for this lesson. If you know that your observer doesn't usually follow a set pattern of questions, check over the rubric and make sure you are offering evidence that supports the highest level of the rubric that you can. For example, if the rubric calls for you to show that you are a recognized leader in planning a certain area, make sure you bring notes from your meetings with colleagues or emails where you took the lead and offered suggestions and resources. If you need to show that students participate, bring copies of student work where kids brainstormed the criteria for the project.

Make sure you provide your documentation and evidence to your observer so it will be available to him or her afterward to clarify any questions or details that may arise from your lesson. Be confident and share the story of your classroom. You are the expert on what happens in that room every day—think of yourself as a tour guide and frame yourself and your students as the community of learners you are.

Avoid Discouragement

In my own experience, in experiences my colleagues have related to me, and in my research for this book, I've come across some discouraging stories regarding observations. One colleague spent over twenty hours preparing for what became an announced observation of a student-driven project: she had gathered multiple data points, put together an entire project plan that included "who struggles and who needs a boost of confidence," and created minilessons to teach students to lead discussions and become session leaders. "When I went into the preconference, I told [the observer] what I wanted her to observe and set up expectations of what [the project] looks like when you're the teacher," she said. The entire lesson was written out, along with data about parent connections and a Google folder of sixteen different Google docs "so [the observer] could get a sense of what [they] had learned and the focus of the unit." She told me, "Everything was super spelled out. I had the Charlotte Danielson template filled in completely." My colleague entered the lesson feeling confident that she had prepared the observer and had demonstrated that she was highly effective in every area. While she received 4s—the highest score—on many points, she got "a few 3s sprinkled in." She thought this was because the observer might not have been comfortable with giving a perfect score, even though my colleague felt she deserved it. Many teachers I spoke with said they felt this was the case at their school—that some administrators have quotas on how many 4s they can (or are willing to) give.

If you suspect that you're facing a system that may not be completely honest about how scores can be distributed, it's tempting to lose faith in the process and to not give it your all. While this is understandable, it won't help you or your students. If you're not happy with the scores the observer offers, you'll need your documentation to make a case for changing the scores. Additionally, the work you're doing in preparing these documents will both prepare you for the observation itself and serve as a helpful reminder to you about your own goals and progress.

Keep Students First

The key to this point in the process is making sure you can explain how every decision relates to student learning. You chose each strategy and skill because of student needs, and when you connect their past learning and performance to your current practice, you show that the students are most important. Without a focus on students, the preconference can feel like a dog and pony show because you are going through the checklist and making sure you covered everything. Instead, I would encourage you to think about this as a chance to check in with yourself on the progress you are making on your personal-growth plan. When we can link every decision we make back to what is best for students, the process becomes less tedious and instead is a way to be certain we are on the right course. Just as we relish seeing our students articulate how they arrived at a solution, we should take pride in our ability to understand our classroom as a challenge to be solved. Because so much of our teaching time is spent in the classroom without an observer, the opportunity to show our commitment to students through our professionalism and expert planning can be our moment to shine.

Date: _____   Class: _____   Observer: _____

	What **strengths** can I discuss in the preconference documents?	What **changes** can I make to improve in this area before the conference? To grow in this area long term?	How will I show my strengths in this area during my **observation lesson**?
Lessons, activities, assignments, experiences I have designed for the students			
What students have learned			
What I have learned			
Routines I've set up for this class			
My own growth this year			

What is my **backup plan** lesson? What materials will I need to have available for that lesson?

Date: _____ Class: _____ Observer: _____

We are focusing on this **content:**

We are focusing on these **skills:**

Our Goals

What will students be able to do as a result of this **lesson**?

How does this lesson fit into this **unit**?

What will students be able to do as a result of this **unit**?

To plan and adjust this lesson and unit, I used:

☐ new professional learning:

☐ student feedback:

☐ student performance:

☐ peer feedback:

☐ my own reflections:

☐ other:

97

Focusing on Students, Not the Observation

It's the day of my scheduled observation. My administrator enters the room. The first thing she sees, in the front row, is a student with her head down and a hood covering her. The other students look at me wide-eyed, but I tell them it is OK and they should get to work. Afterward, my administrator asks why I allowed a student to sleep in class. My answer is simple: "She had a note from the nurse that there's a family emergency. The counselors are at a meeting and the nurse doesn't have room for her to stay there, so we are being asked to let her be until someone can pick her up."

If we look at this situation logically, it doesn't seem very newsworthy: the observer wondered about something she saw, and I explained what happened. However, if this had happened earlier in my career, I would have been rattled. I would have felt the need to take time during class to tell the observer what had happened, or I might have asked a neighboring teacher if my student could sit in that class during the observation.

Often, we consider an observation to be a kind of performance in which there is no room for unplanned or untidy elements. In truth, good teaching is not something we do for an observer's entertainment, and it rarely looks like the well-choreographed scenes in movies about teachers. It's the everyday work of helping each of our students to reach their potential. Observers can and should see what the day-to-day realities of our classrooms are like. It is up to us to put less pressure on ourselves to make observed lessons perfect and put more emphasis on making sure we are doing the best we can by each student in the room.

Being observed can be stressful for even the most experienced teacher. Many amazing teachers get stage fright when an outsider is present in the classroom. This chapter is about setting yourself up for success in your observation. Instead of new pages for your journal, this chapter includes strategies you can use immediately to be prepared for your next observation and to document what happens during the lesson. By using these strategies, you can keep your focus where it really matters: on students rather than on the observer.

Acknowledge the Observer and Make Students Comfortable

It's happened to all of us: Someone walks into the room, and your normally engaged class clams up. Or the quietest kids start yammering loudly on something completely off topic.

Administrator Damian Bariexca says that as a teacher, and now as an administrator, he finds it best to introduce the observer and say something about how the observer is there to see the good work students are doing. Letting the observer smile and wave in response to this introduction "normalizes the environment."

While I have heard about situations in which teachers have framed the observation in more dire terms, that approach doesn't convey a focus on students. Also, it may have a negative effect: "My first year, I [told the class] a person was coming to observe them and check their behavior," explained one middle school teacher. "It backfired. They just sat there and then afterward asked, 'How did we do?'"

Lisa Sidorick-Weise, a colleague of mine who teaches special education students, is acutely aware of how the presence of another adult in the room affects her students. "I tell them in advance, if I know," she explained to me, adding that some students have missed days of school rather than be in class on a day when she was expecting a visitor. Lisa's constant focus on her students is an approach that works in mainstream classes as well as special education classes. "I introduce every adult who comes in my room for any reason to try to get my students comfortable with teachers they don't have or may have. The most important thing for my special education students is to be clear that I'm here for them, no matter what. They are going to supersede anyone who's in this room." Finally, keeping the day as normal as possible for students will help them to behave as they typically do and will help the observer get a better idea of what your work looks like. Rely on the routines and classroom norms you've established.

Keep Your Focus on Your Students

While being observed can be distracting or even nerve-racking, you don't have to let it get you off your game. Some planning ahead will help you be prepared and stay present in the lesson with your students. Most of the evaluation rubrics are focused on helping students learn, so when we stay with our students in the learning, we not only keep the learning on track rather than lose a day of instruction but also do better in our observed lesson.

Classrooms are often filled with a lot of sound and movement, and it is easy for both the teacher and the observer to miss all that happens simultaneously. Administrator Damian Bariexca suggests, when possible, inviting the observer to engage in the activity with the students. This, he says, helps both the teacher and the students feel more calm and less like they are being observed. "Whether it's a discussion or a hands-on lesson, being actively involved gives us the best chance to see the classroom from the students' perspective. (Plus, it's fun!)."

The following is a list of things to consider when preparing for the lesson. Because the first observation is usually an announced one, you should have time to arrange the learning environment to help you and the students stay focused and unflustered. Making these kinds of preparations part of your everyday routine will help your days run more smoothly and will help you during unannounced observations, as well.

Overall, maintain your **focus on student engagement**. When someone else is in the room, it's easy to spend more time thinking about what you're going to say or what you're doing. When you step back and monitor student engagement, the entire lesson flows better and students aren't as nervous either.

Have routines and norms in place to **be prepared for disruptions**: emergency drills, announcements during a discussion, a bee that enters the room and incites panic, visitors dropping by to ask if they can borrow something or have a student for a few minutes. Letting students know that you recognize the disruption and expect them to respond appropriately shows that you are thinking about them rather than the observer.

Think about what you leave out of your lessons most often, and make sure you **post visual cues for yourself**. Here are a few just-for-me cues that I rely on in my classroom (see also Figure 7.1):

- I know that when I get flustered, I forget what time the class period ends. On my lectern I have taped down the **bell schedule** for regular days, early dismissals, and delayed openings.

- In my district's evaluation and in my practice, questioning is a focus area, so I have **question stems and levels** taped on the lectern too. When I use these stems, it's easy for an observer to follow the structure of my questioning.

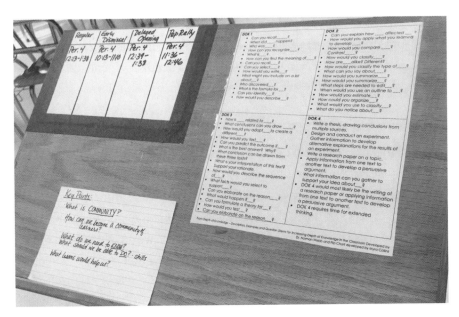

Figure 7.1 Even if I don't refer to the cues I have left for myself during an observed lesson, knowing they're there if I need them helps me feel calm.

- My **essential questions for the unit and the guiding questions for the lesson** are always posted on the whiteboard. I sometimes write down discussion questions I want to ask and keep those on the lectern, as well.

- I keep a **checklist of the key elements I am including in the lesson** on my lectern, too, when I know I'm being observed. This is just a list of the key ideas I need to make sure I hit.

Anchor charts provide another way for you and for students to keep focused during an observed lesson. Anchor charts are big posters that I create with students during instruction and then hang up so that we can refer to them throughout subsequent lessons. They capture learning while it happens. Using an anchor chart helps me to remember all of the facets of the work we're doing. For example, I teach eight elements of character, but when put on the spot, it takes me a few minutes to figure out which one I'm inevitably forgetting. Tying the current lesson to past learning is easy with an anchor chart. Creating an anchor chart during an observed lesson makes the learning interactive, shows you intend to connect this lesson to future lessons, and helps keep everyone focused, including the observer.

Of course, there's no way that I'm going to refer to every single one of these tools while I am teaching. However, if I have a moment of uncertainty while I'm being observed, I know exactly where to look for quick help, without interrupting the lesson. Just knowing that I have these tools in place if I need them lets me focus on my students without worrying about extraneous details.

Take Notes

Another tool that helps me stay focused while I'm being observed is a notepad or clipboard that I leave out to jot down ideas and my own observations, especially on student engagement. After my evaluation, I tuck my notes into my professional development journal. The notes I take during the evaluation are quick, and they might not make sense to anyone but me. However, they are a great help to me when I am reflecting on the observation, writing my postobservation notes, and explaining my work during the postobservation conference.

Before the observer comes, I think about where that person will likely sit, usually near an outlet. Then I figure out what is hard to see and to hear from there so I can be more aware of those places during the lesson. During the class, if there is something happening in those locations that I'll want to bring to the observer's attention, I jot it down.

The notepad also comes in handy for taking notes about any adjustments I make. If a student asks a question that presents a teachable moment that doesn't take us too far afield, I make a note of what the question is and a few words of my response in case the observer doesn't hear the original question. Perhaps while they are in small groups, I notice several groups have misunderstood the directions. I will make a note of that and either adjust the lesson to accommodate what they understood the directions to mean or call the class back together to clarify expectations, but I also make a note of which students I am responding to. In my postconference, I will be able to show I made those adjustments with specific evidence from my students.

Snippets of good conversation among students, moments that capture the goals of the lesson, or other noteworthy student responses are also helpful to jot down when they are happening. I make note of these not only to help my evaluation but also so I can show in my postconference how I will use these observed comments to further student learning in my next lessons. Most evaluation models ask not only what adjustments were made to the observed lesson but also how you will modify future lessons based on today. Student questions are an excellent start to adjusting future plans.

Your impressions and memories immediately after the lesson will also be valuable. In Chapter 8, you'll find some guidance about what to note, as well as a journal page (8.01) for recording your thinking.

Change Course if It's Not Going Well

Having an observer in the room doesn't just make us nervous—sometimes it changes student behavior, too. Students become too strident in calling others out for misbehavior. Otherwise well-behaved students decide to make themselves the center of attention for all the wrong reasons. And all of the minor disruptions that could happen on any day are just as likely to happen on an observation day. What do you do when a lesson isn't going the way you had hoped? Here are some strategies.

Do a Quick Formative Assessment

Stop the class and ask everyone to do one sample problem or quick write, and circulate to watch the strategies students use. If you are working on something that requires background knowledge, do a quick check of that. Keep blank sheets for quick formative assessments handy. Next, ask students to gauge their understanding using a five-finger check-in (where they hold up the number of fingers that best describes their grasp of the topic, with one being not at all and five meaning they could teach it to someone else), or ask students to explain the directions to someone near them. Find a way to see where the plans went wrong.

Think About What Students Need

Ask yourself, "What do my students need to get back on track?" The answer is likely that they need more information, more time, or clearer directions. If students need more time, can you eliminate some steps or have a group check-in before continuing? If only a few groups need to be addressed, let the other groups keep working and either address the struggling groups one at a time or, if the topic is more complicated, pull the groups who need more assistance together and give them more information or refine the directions.

Give Yourself a Moment to Think

If you aren't sure how to fix what is happening and you need a few moments to think it through, stop the class and ask students to write a reflection on what the directions were, what steps they are following, what progress they feel they are making, and what they need to complete the task successfully. While they are writing, brainstorm ways you can fix the problem. How can you help students reach your lesson objectives in the time remaining? If the problem, for example, is that the groups are off task and not working on what they are supposed to be doing, perhaps you can have students complete the reflection, share with someone near them (if you can do it without more disruption), and offer suggestions to the class for working together better. If you don't think you can salvage groups or you don't have enough time, ask students to complete part of what they were doing together independently and tell them they will reconvene tomorrow to review how to use their individual contributions in groups the following day.

Breathe

If you are noticing signs of stress or panic in yourself during this process, take a minute to clear your head. While students are working on the quick recall or reflection activity you gave them, breathe deeply. Count to ten (or twenty). Our students reflect our energy back to us: if we get stressed and speak abruptly to students, we're likely to get the same (or worse) back. Remember that the observer in the room has been in your position and understands that these things happen. You aren't being scored on whether everything goes perfectly; you're being scored on how you handle the unexpected.

Go to Plan B

If you notice a lesson is not working early enough (or some segment isn't working) and you can't salvage it, say something like, "Sorry, class, I misjudged what we were ready for. Let's back up and try this instead," while you hand out the new directions. If it is appropriate, tell them you'll come back to the original activity another time. What is most important in your observation is that you realized things weren't working and responded in a way that you can explain.

High school biology teacher Russell Whaley said he ended up getting a good score during an observation even though, in the middle of his lesson, the technology completely shut down. Rather than try to get the projector to come back on, he continued writing on the board as if nothing had happened, and his seamless transition to a nontechnological solution showed that his focus was on student learning. This is also a good reminder to always have a backup plan for technology. I've learned—especially in my film class, which would otherwise be derailed when the projector stopped working—to always have a list of discussion topics that are relevant to what we are learning ready to go.

Keep Students First

Having someone else in our classroom can throw off students and us. Remember to connect with students individually throughout the class period: greet them at the door and check in with how they are feeling and what is happening. Listen to their responses rather than getting caught up in what your follow-up question will be. Be curious about your students and their ideas, their way of thinking about things; it will help you stay focused on what matters: helping your students grow. In short, being present with our students is the best gift we can give them, especially when observers can make them feel uncomfortable in our classes.

Planning for the Postobservation Conference

The bell rings to end class, and my students pack up and file out, saying goodbye to their classmates and to me. The administrator in the back of the room thanks me and leaves, telling me we will meet in two days to discuss the observation. But before I breathe a sigh of relief and relax, I need to take a few steps to be best prepared for my postobservation conference. It's human to want to just get on with the day as soon as an evaluation is over. I know many teachers who say they don't think about their observation again until they sit down with their administrators. But if the administrators who are writing up the evaluations are going to spend time thinking about what to say at the postobservation conference, we should do the same.

So often, we don't give ourselves credit for what we do in the classroom, focusing on all the things we need to improve rather than celebrating what we have achieved. The postobservation moment is a time to put ourselves in the position of an outsider and have a conversation with ourselves about our lesson planning, our classroom practice, and our students. When we're done, we will have an outside party give us another viewpoint to compare with the ideas we have, but in this moment of reflection, we should devote time to our own successes and our students' growth.

We can also take this chance to consider our own thinking about ourselves and our students and reconsider the plans we made when we started the year. The map and the journey are not the same, and postobservation reflections give us a chance to change the destination or revise the route.

Before You Relax: Take a Few Quick Steps Right After the Observation

These first moments are critical. Before your memories get mixed together with memories of other students, other lessons, and other conversations, you need to collect the details of the classroom experience for the lesson that was observed.

Take Notes

In the few minutes before the next class begins, I grab a notepad and stand in my doorway to greet students, furiously making notes about what happened during class. My first goal is to capture the fleeting moments that might need to be contextualized for an outside observer: the student who struggles with peer relationships who loaned another student a pen, the question a student asked on his way out that showed he was completely engaged with the topic, and so on.

The notes that I make in these moments will help me show my administrator how what she saw today fits into the larger picture of this class as a whole. When an observer sits in our classrooms only once or twice a year, it is the equivalent of watching a single episode of a serialized television drama without knowing what has come before. My husband occasionally wanders through when I'm watching *Downton Abbey*, and although he'll appreciate the dowager countess' wit, when he notes the tension between Lady Edith and Lady Mary, he has no idea that it relates to carrying a dead Turk's body out of the house many seasons ago. While he can watch one episode and notice strong acting or writing or even foreshadowing, he doesn't fully understand the relationships between the characters or why certain comments or events are significant. In the same way, even a smart and well-meaning administrator might not understand the nuances of the interactions in your classroom: you have to give him or her the **context to show what's really happening**. I have seen many notes on observations that said, "Student asked a question, and teacher said . . ." While factually accurate, such a note doesn't show why my response was both appropriate and helpful for the student. I've had observers assume that whispering students were off task, but I heard them discussing the assignment. What meaningful interaction might your observer have *not* heard? Jot those moments down.

Those immediate moments after the observation are also when I make note of any **adjustments I made to my original plans**. It is more important that we adjust to give kids what they

See Professional Journal Page 8.01 at the end of this chapter for a reproducible list of prompts.

(Also available online as a digital download.)

English teacher Sarah Mulhern Gross explained how she reflects immediately after an observation: "I try to write down ideas immediately after the observation, even if it's just in my own shorthand. I like to ask myself what I will change for the next group, too. Sometimes things need to change before I do the lesson again next year. Even if it's only a little change, I like to think about what will work best for each of my four sections."

need in a class, even when it's an observation day, than to stick rigidly with our original plan. We can always explain to the observer why we made this decision.

This is also the time to jot down any **incidents or circumstances that may have affected the lesson**: the student who got sick and had to leave the room, the call for a student for early dismissal that left a group one short before their presentation. All these things, from minor schedule disruptions to major life events, impact instruction in ways we can't plan for. It's easy to forget that we need to explain them because, unfortunately, they happen all the time.

One year during my observation, I noticed that a group of boys who had previously been excited about participating in readers theatre now seemed sullen. They lacked their usual energy. I crouched down in front of one the boys and asked what was happening. He told me that another student's grandmother had died, which I knew. What I had not realized was that *all* the boys were close to her: she had been making their after-school snacks and picking them up from practices for years. I made a quick change to my plans and added a writing activity to the start of class that allowed students to write about their feelings. Giving them a few minutes with their own thoughts didn't magically make them forget their sadness, but honoring their grief was more important than delivering the lesson I'd written. During my postobservation conference, I explained why I'd departed from my plans, and the evaluator understood that I was meeting student needs.

It's easy to get lost in our own concerns when we are being observed. We need to remember that for students, our observation days are still learning days.

Take Pictures

If possible, snap a few photos of the room at the end of class: Capture whatever is on the whiteboard, how students were grouped, anchor charts. Document the setup of supplies for a lab or the organization of manipulatives in math. If students own classroom procedures such as distributing supplies or returning papers, take photos of those systems. The environment you've created in your classroom and the tools that you've built into it are part of the students' experience in your room. However, observers don't know the room as well as you do: I've had observers miss that the agenda was posted, for example, or that guiding questions were listed on the board. These photos will also come in handy later when you are trying to recall the class in more detail (especially for those of us who teach multiple sections of the same class—it's easy to forget what happened during third period when you taught the lesson five times that day!).

Before You Dive In: Reframe the Upcoming Conference

In the conversations I had with teachers about their evaluations while I was writing this book, I often heard an undercurrent of skepticism about the systems by which they were being evaluated. One teacher I spoke to said that he'd had three different administrators observe him and in the process experienced three different interpretations of the rubric. Some were more about coaching to get better while others were looking for faults. Another told me that she will ask questions of some administrators but not of others, depending on her relationship with each person. If she doesn't feel that she has a strong relationship with the observer, she feels unsure whether the administrator is criticizing because there is a real issue with her work or because the observer might have done it differently.

These concerns aren't new. As early as 1985, Madeline Hunter complained that her teacher evaluation model was being misused because evaluators were looking for the way they would have applied it in their classrooms years before. "Instead, [administrators] need to become expert in translation of theory into practice in order to help teachers use their own styles to achieve excellence," Hunter wrote (60). "In addition, administrators need to internalize skills to become models for teachers. Otherwise, a do-as-I-say-not-as-I-do situation exists" (60). The disconnect between our expectations of the system and our observers' expectations of the system can be frustrating to both sides.

If we feel that we are at the mercy of a system, it's not surprising that we might distrust it. However, administrator Damian Bariexca reminds us to consider how it might not be the system, but a difference in perspective that is to blame. He asks, "How do you and your administrator view the evaluation process? Is it another to-do box to check off, or is it an opportunity to engage in meaningful dialogue about the process of teaching and learning? Speaking of dialogue, is it really a dialogue or is it a monologue? In the postobservation conference, does the administrator approach from a deficit model ('Here's what you need to improve'), an encouragement model ('I really liked X and encourage you to continue doing that'), or a combination of both? Is the observation process an opportunity to hear feedback to help you improve your craft, or is it a weapon?"

Damian has a few suggestions for bridging this gap in expectations: "In a perfect world, we would always get the feedback we want from the process (don't forget, administrators get evaluated, too). In the real world, however, sometimes we have to ask for what we want. Don't be afraid to ask your observer for feedback that you will find helpful. 'What did you see that I should do more of?' 'How can I improve upon X?' Even if the administrator is not an expert in your content area, [he or she] should be able to give you suggestions about pedagogy that you can then apply to your discipline or your specific classroom." As you think about your lesson, consider the relationship you have with the observer and what feedback would be most useful for you going forward.

As you write the documentation that will help your observer see your work within the structure of your evaluation model, also consider these questions: What do *you* want from the postobservation conference? How can you make your perspective clearer to your observer?

When You Have Time: Assess Your Performance Against the Standards

Later that day, if possible, but at least before the postobservation conference, I grab a mug of hot tea and settle in with my preobservation conference notes and plans, a copy of the evaluation rubric, examples of evidence for each indicator or element, and a notepad. While many evaluation models have lists of postobservation questions, I don't start with those. I first go through my notes and look at where *I* see evidence for where I have met the criteria of the standards.

As you work through the standards, consider the lesson from three angles: the lesson as a stand-alone experience, the lesson in the context of the larger unit, and the lesson as it relates to the students. Make notes organized by the sections of the evaluation model so you can refer back to them during the postobservation conference. Or, use Professional Journal Page 8.02 and add annotations about which section of the model each note addresses. Taking time to think through these ideas helps keep the students as the focus of your planning and reflection. As you make your notes, use the language of the standards. Doing so makes it easy for the evaluator to identify the key words that are separate levels on the evaluation rubric.

Also take time to reflect on the lesson itself: What went particularly well? What would you change next time? Why? Why did you make the decisions you made, and what else had you considered? Be specific here when possible. Perhaps you would have grouped students differently or they needed more (or less) time to complete a task. Maybe you would have stopped partway through to review the steps. The more specifically you can analyze and reflect on each part of your lesson, the more you'll be able to articulate your decisions and offer proof of your ability to think deeply about your practice, rather than present yourself as someone who attempts strategies randomly without considering why or how effectively they work. Damian notes, "As an evaluator, I love to see that teachers are reflecting on their practice and making adjustments for future lessons. It may not be necessary to do it in the heat of the moment, but do take the time to reflect on specific elements for tweaking or improving, not just broad, general statements." I often do this reflection work right on my lesson plans and then copy it as part of my postconference artifacts.

Now consider how much of what you noted was visible to your observer. Where will you need more evidence to help the person doing the evaluation see that you've done what you set out to do? You might, as middle school English language arts teacher Kelly Kosch does, photocopy student work to bring to the postobservation conference so that you can show the evaluator evidence of students' gains. Also consider how the photos you took earlier might help an evaluator see the full picture of the work you're doing with this class. Shots of tools for students that you've embedded in your classroom environment, such as anchor charts or essential questions, show that you're supporting students.

See Professional Journal Page 8.02 at the end of this chapter for a reproducible for reflecting on your lesson.

(Also available online as a digital download.)

The Most Important Step: Reflect on Your Successes

It might seem like the next step after checking the standards and noting evidence would be to leap into whatever postobservation conference form you are required to fill out, if any. However, I invite you to first consider the reflective questions here and to take some time to linger on what went right during the observation lesson.

Many teachers find the time between the end of the observation and the delivery of "judgment" at the postobservation conference to be the hardest part of the evaluation process. Strong teachers agonize over their performance, wondering what their evaluation will bring and how the observer perceived their performance. If we choose to view the postobservation conference as a judgment, we are allowing someone else to define who we are as teachers. We are giving up our power.

In reality, this is not a powerless moment. Approaching the conference with an eye to what we've done well, we can provide more evidence of our strengths, explain how we've met students' needs, show how we made adjustments, and explain where subsequent lessons went. As the expert voice of what happens in our classrooms daily, we owe it to ourselves to be just as well prepared—if not more so—than the observer and to form our own opinions of our performance independent of the observer's opinion.

The following questions form the backbone of how I approach the postobservation conference:

What Excited You About the Lesson?

Thinking about what excited you about the lesson guides you to consider why you chose this path and how the students responded to it. Which students exceeded your expectations for the lesson? How do you know? Which students met those expectations? Where is the evidence of that? In considering this question, even seemingly small details can be powerful: During one evaluation, my students entered the classroom and began discussing their books authentically, giving quick reviews and offering insights such as that a book was tough to get into but worth it for the ending. When I began the

8.03

See Professional Journal Page 8.03 at the end of this chapter for a reproducible journaling page.

(Also available online as a digital download.)

postobservation conference by saying I was thrilled that I entered the classroom to see students engaged in conversations about books, it brought the evaluator back to that moment and prompted her to read me the comments she had documented from the students. Starting the conversation on that positive note let me segue to something students had spent months developing.

Inevitably, the first question of a postobservation conference is "How do you think the lesson went?" Thinking about what excited you about the lesson and where you're seeing student success gives you a way to present the lesson positively with strong evidence rather than just saying, "I think it went well," and then deferring to the observer's assessment.

How Does This Lesson Show Your Own Learning?

What did you do in this lesson that was new, revised, or retooled from a past lesson? Did you apply a strategy you learned about in a workshop? Create a new set of questions to challenge students? Evidence of your own professional growth also matters when you think about how you are evaluated, and how you think about yourself as a learner and model that for your students make a difference in your classroom.

What Resources Did You Use to Prepare the Lesson?

Take a moment to consider, name, and take pride in your own professional knowledge. In some evaluation models, teachers need to demonstrate their knowledge of professional resources. If the observer in your room is not familiar with your content area, you may need to call attention to the research and resources you are using. Even the best observer may need help with taking in everything that happens in the class. Middle school English language arts teacher Denise Weintraut recalled when an administrator whose area of expertise was in a different content area did not understand the importance and relevance of a lesson she taught her struggling readers on paying attention to voice. "She had started marking me down for the lesson, saying, 'I don't think this was a worthwhile thing to teach,'" Weintraut recalled. "The way I got her around to my way of thinking was to quote experts, to say, 'This is from the work of Cris Tovani.' I had to work hard to educate her. . . . I turned it around in the postobservation conference because I was able to quote research that supported the value of what I was doing."

How Can You Push Students to Achieve Something Even Bigger than Originally Planned?

Our evaluation can be a reminder to think about how we can help students dream bigger and achieve more. If you are working on memoir, can you help them connect with community members to create digital stories for senior citizens to share with their grandchildren? If you are reading a novel about animals, can you find a real-world connection to video conference with, such as a biologist or someone from the zoo? When my students started following the aftermath of Superstorm Sandy, which affected our area, I looked for ways to help them put their energy to good use. Several of them reached out to local grassroots charities and got involved, creating social media videos for those charities to use on their websites to raise awareness.

Gather Evidence

Once I have my notes aligned with the evaluation rubric and I have thought about both student learning and my learning, I find the evidence I need for each section. I compile artifacts I have and list anything I need to pull from student work folders or get copies of from student notebooks.

If a lesson came out of a perceived need, you might photocopy student work that shows that students were struggling with a concept. If you need to show classroom procedures, you might have photos of posters explaining the procedures or copies of handouts that you used when you taught the procedures. Make copies of student reflections from lessons prior or the lesson that was observed. If you finish a unit reflection that includes the observed lesson before the postobservation conference, take copies of those, too. When selecting student work, focus not on the "perfect" answers, but the ones that show learning and growth. A student who struggles but reflects on that struggle and has a plan to fix it might be a better exemplar of student engagement than a student who is always at the top of the class. Often, we feel pressure to show off what our best students can do, but if those students would be performing at that level without our instruction, it may be more beneficial to showcase student work that demonstrates a learning curve where you can point to specific lessons and instruction that raised students' awareness of different elements.

In addition to evidence of student learning, make copies of the tools you use for gathering that evidence. If you use a student reflection sheet at the end of the unit, include it to show how you are monitoring student growth and agency. If you use facilitation grids—tables to track student progress or participation, in which each student has a row and each criterion or step has a column (see sample, page 117)—include those as evidence of learning and ongoing assessment. If students are keeping logs of their own reading, make copies of their logs as well as any class logs that are circulated daily to show that students are involved in keeping their own records but that you also have a strategy that allows you to see at a glance how students are doing. If you have students keep learning logs of math problems or science concepts, those artifacts show that you are systematic in both how you have students reflect and how you collect information.

Because I have students reflect on their learning so often, I occasionally ask them for copies of their reflections from their notebooks. Whether it is a quick write on what they learned, a reflection essay, an inventory that shows growth using a scale or temperature gauge, or a double-entry journal, these student reflections provide important insight into the learning process and my classroom procedures that is valuable for me and for the evaluator. When students habitually track their understanding through reflection, it allows us to dip into the river of student learning at any point, whether for our evaluations or for classroom instruction.

Complete the Postobservation Documents

For many evaluation models, there are postobservation documents for both you and the observer to prepare for the postobservation meeting. The observer uses these, along with the preobservation documents, as evidence when writing up the observation. It's often common practice for teachers' notes to be cut and pasted directly into the final evaluation document. Using the language of the scoring rubric in your document will help the observer to find the language he or she needs to express how you have excelled in the areas the rubric measures.

While working through the questions on the documents, refer back to your preobservation conference forms and notes, the standards, the scoring rubric, and the notes in which you documented how you addressed the elements of the scoring rubric. With all those documents as your prewriting, your answers to the postobservation questions will be more cogent and supported with evidence, with copies where appropriate. Your copies of pertinent artifacts—prompts, mentor texts, graphic organizers, and student logs—also belong in the postobservation conference documents. Try to do the following as you write.

Make Your Instructional Design Obvious

Your instructional design matters: refer to your essential questions and objectives or goals for the lesson along with the evidence that you achieved them. Make sure the observer can clearly follow your thinking.

What Evidence Might You Include in the Documentation for Your Postobservation Conference?

The following shows some of the evidence I put together for a single postobservation conference. What I actually show to my observer during the postobservation conference will likely be a curated selection that best represents the work done by me and by the students. However, I submit all the artifacts to give the observer as much evidence and context as possible.

The artifacts shown here document an observed lesson that asked students to collaborate in small groups to analyze a version of a scene from Shakespeare's *Much Ado About Nothing*.

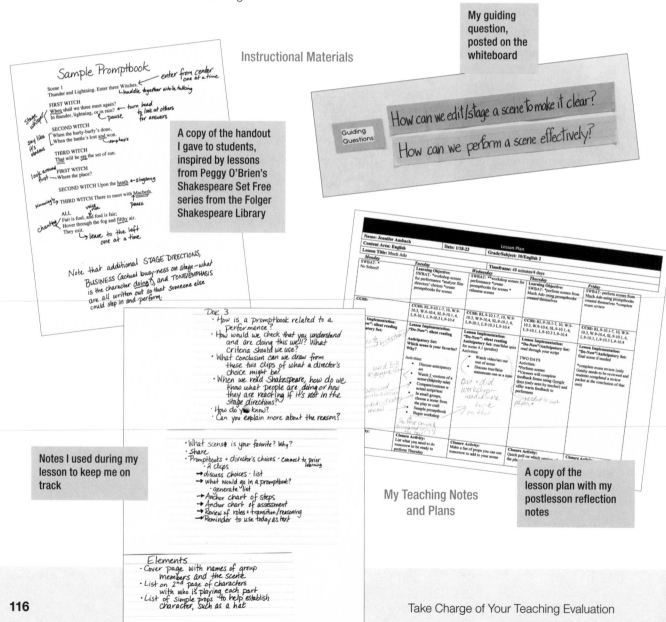

Instructional Materials

My guiding question, posted on the whiteboard

A copy of the handout I gave to students, inspired by lessons from Peggy O'Brien's Shakespeare Set Free series from the Folger Shakespeare Library

Notes I used during my lesson to keep me on track

My Teaching Notes and Plans

A copy of the lesson plan with my postlesson reflection notes

Evaluation Tools

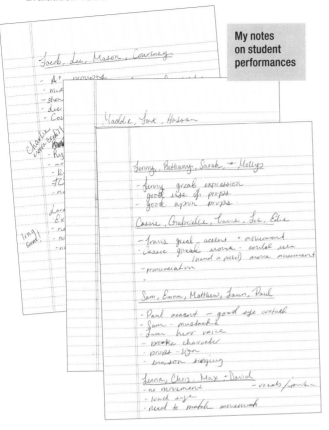

My notes on student performances

Planning Notes for the Postobservation Conference

My notes about the class and how the lesson aligned with each element of the evaluation rubric

Student reflections on other groups' performances and their own group performance

The facilitation grid I used for tracking student group work

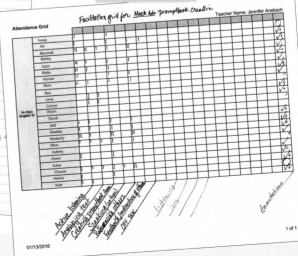

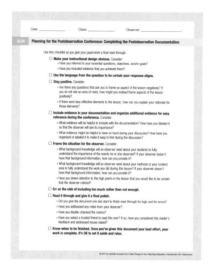

See Professional Journal Page 8.04 at the end of this chapter for a reproducible version of these reminders for your professional development journal.

(Also available online as a digital download.)

Use the Language from the Question

Align your responses with the language of the evaluation to ensure that the observer sees the same connections between your work and the evaluation criteria that you see.

Stay Positive

When a question asks for examples of elements of instruction that were "effective" and "less effective," it suggests that part of the lesson proved less effective. However, in a given lesson, there may not be elements that were less effective. Instead, focus on how engaging the strategies you used were. If there were elements that were less effective (a poem didn't spark the connections you thought it would, for example), take time to explain the evidence you used in selecting that piece as something students would engage in ("Because students found other poems by Billy Collins to be full of connections to this unit, I thought this poem would provide an engaging transition to the next unit") to show that you are an expert at what you do. No one can predict exactly how students will respond, but providing a rationale for your choice shows that you are doing the work required to be a reflective educator.

Include Organized Evidence in Your Documentation

Organize all evidence for easy reference during the postobservation conference. Submit pertinent artifacts, labeled with sticky notes to help your observer see how they fit into the larger framework of the observation ("This is the work from the student you spoke to in the front of the room"). If you have student work and reflections from subsequent lessons, consider including them to show further evidence of addressing the essential questions, since those often involve multiple lessons. In addition, I always have pieces with me that I won't necessarily submit but have on hand in case the observer asks a question about something. If you love binders, as I do, by all means, put them in a binder. I use small sticky notes as tabs, sometimes labeled with the domain element or with notes to remind myself why I selected particular artifacts. This allows me to access pieces quickly should I need to during my postobservation conference.

Frame the Situation for the Observer

Oftentimes, outside visitors—even experts—can misinterpret what they are seeing because our strategies are different from what they have seen before or because they don't know the full history of our work with this class. Consider the postobservation documents to be your chance to give the guided tour of your lesson, stopping to point out interesting bits along the way and showing your expertise at analyzing what you see.

Err on the Side of Too Much Rather than Not Enough

While it may feel tedious to write out long documents, especially when you've already put a lot of effort into the preobservation conference documents, the more evidence you supply, the more evidence the observer can include in your evaluation. Add details, anecdotes, and background information. Mention the workshop you took or the book you read to discover a new practice you incorporated into the lesson. Be thorough and don't just connect the dots for your observer—place those dots close together so your design, strategies, assessments, and environment reflect a coherent picture without too much effort on the part of an outsider. Think about it like constellations: you don't want the observer to see the Big Dipper when you wanted him or her to see the Great Bear.

Read It Through and Give It a Final Polish

Take a moment to flip back through your preconference notes. Did you set up anything that you forgot to touch on, whether to provide evidence of what you did or to explain why you omitted it? If you have notes from your observer, go back through those carefully after you have done your own work and make sure you have addressed anything the observer didn't notice, whether you need to write a response or provide evidence of student achievement. Double-check the rubrics and language. Did you provide evidence of things that might not have been observable but you can still document? Proofread for errors and, if you are comfortable, ask a trusted friend to read it over and give you feedback on where you may be unclear or could include something else.

Know When to Be Finished

In my work as a reporter before I became a teacher, I absorbed the newspaper mantra "It's not done; it's due." In the past, I carried this practice over to my work on my evaluations: I learned to finish all of the major components for my postobservation conference before the deadline, but I continued to work on my pieces until the deadline hit, changing wording, finding one more document, one more example, one more student reflection. While this approach makes for dramatic moments in the newspaper world, it isn't necessary for this work. If you have worked through the steps in this chapter, addressed the rubrics and any gaps in the notes from the observer, and provided evidence where possible, your work is complete.

When the Lesson Didn't Go Well: Find the Positives

Sometimes, despite our best plans, a lesson does not go as anticipated. At these moments, it is easy to throw up your hands and declare the entire lesson a disaster.

However, expert teachers rarely have lessons that are that far off the mark. And if you're reading this book, you're clearly a teacher who cares about your practice and your students. So what do you do next?

First, *jot down all the notes you can* immediately afterward—the conversations, the students who seemed off, the questions that arose, the technology that didn't work, the student responses that didn't fit your expectations. Collect as much student work as possible, including students' notes. If, during the lesson, you headed off an issue by asking students to write on-the-spot reflections (as discussed in Chapter 7), gather that student writing as well.

Later, when you've had a chance to shake off any initial disappointment about the lesson, take a moment to *step back and look at your goals and the evaluation model*. Certainly, you have evidence of achievement of many of those elements. Remember, no one expects students to be perfect. Instead, your goal is to show that you designed appropriate lessons and goals based on the evidence you had and that your feedback to students was appropriate and consistent. Then, work through the process outlined earlier in this chapter, keeping in mind the strengths that you demonstrated in the observed lesson.

A few years ago, I was observed during a lesson I'd prepared to help one of my tenth-grade classes learn to work collaboratively after seeing them struggle with the social skills involved. The students worked cooperatively in their small groups, but when they needed to find other resources, trouble began. I stopped the lesson at two points and asked students to consider if they were achieving their goals, if they were applying the guiding questions to their work, and if they could get a better outcome by changing what they were doing. Despite this, students devolved into arguing. I had them clean up, return to their seats, and write their reflections on premade exit slips. Then we had a group discussion on what had happened.

It seemed like a disaster.

However, when I read the students' exit slips later and looked at the goals and the evaluation rubric, I realized that I *had* achieved the goal. Students had articulated what they needed to do and had identified their frustrations. They brainstormed ways they could have completed the activity differently to be efficient. Their exit slips showed that they could identify what they needed to do to be a team and how important communication was. All students engaged in the lesson, and during the debriefing, they asked each other questions and worked to find the answers they needed.

It was a great relief to realize that the lesson had truly been meaningful and helpful for students, and I began thinking of how we might build on these gains in future lessons relating to social skills. While it would have been tidy for the sake of the observation if the students had all had an epiphany and worked together in harmony in the lesson, I had documentation that showed that my goals for the students were appropriate and that the students were making progress toward them.

We need to be mindful of how we talk to ourselves about what happens in our classrooms. Wanting to be a better teacher and thinking about teaching practice sets us on the right path. Being unnecessarily harsh on ourselves is not helpful to us or our students. We can talk to ourselves the way we speak to our students: It was just one lesson. We can recover from this. What parts of what we're doing are going well? Where should we start to make improvements tomorrow?

Keep Students First

The work we did together in this chapter was about gathering evidence and validating your performance. While you might find some excitement in the intellectual challenges this exercise provides, you didn't become a teacher to argue. When you're done preparing for the postobservation conference, keep your focus on what matters most: the students. Skim over the photos, especially if they contain students working. Flip back through the student work you collected. Consider how you can support those who struggled with this lesson. Cheer for those students who, up against so many daily challenges, come to school and learn what they can. Rather than worrying about what someone else thought of what happened in the classroom, think about what you learn from your students each day. The work we do matters, and taking a step back to appreciate the group of students before us can shift our entire perception of our day. This can be a moment of celebration, of noticing the incremental steps students make, and of being grateful for our role in this formative period of their lives.

Date: _____   Class: _____   Observer: _____

Interruptions or Unusual Circumstances to Address:

From the Students: Important Comments, Great Questions, and Positive Interactions:

The next time I teach this lesson,
I'll . . .

Artifacts to Include in My
Documentation:

Date: _____   Class: _____   Observer: _____

I know that this lesson is helpful to students because . . .

These formative **assessments** indicate that the lesson is helpful for students:	Students **showed growth and learning** by . . .	I kept students **engaged** by . . .

I know that this lesson is important to the unit overall because . . .

It helped my students, as individuals, by . . .

continues   **123**

I know that this lesson is a good fit for the students in this class because . . .

My work in this lesson facilitated students' social and emotional growth in these ways:

It built on these previous lessons and assessments:	It drew on the following skills that students learned earlier in the unit or year:	It prepared students for these lessons and summative evaluations:

Date: _____   Class: _____   Observer: _____

Here's what was exciting
about this lesson:

In this lesson, I showed my own
learning by . . .

Based on this lesson, I think
I can push my students to something
even bigger than I'd originally planned.
Here's what I have in mind:

I used these resources to create the lesson:

8.04 **Planning for the Postobservation Conference: Completing the Postobservation Documentation**

Use this checklist as you give your paperwork a final read-through.

☐ **Make your instructional design obvious.** Consider:
- Have you referred to your essential questions, objectives, and/or goals?
- Have you included evidence that you achieved them?

☐ **Use the language from the question to be certain your response aligns.**

☐ **Stay positive.** Consider:
- Are there any questions that ask you to frame an aspect of the lesson negatively? If you do not see an area of need, how might you instead frame aspects of the lesson positively?
- If there were less-effective elements to the lesson, how can you explain your rationale for those elements?

☐ **Include evidence in your documentation and organize additional evidence for easy reference during the conference.** Consider:
- What evidence will be helpful to include with the documentation? How have you labeled it so that the observer will see its importance?
- What evidence might be helpful to have on hand during your discussion? How have you organized or labeled it to make it easy to find during the discussion?

☐ **Frame the situation for the observer.** Consider:
- What background knowledge will an observer need about your students to fully understand the importance of the events he or she observed? If your observer doesn't have that background information, how can you provide it?
- What background knowledge will an observer need about your methods or your content area to fully understand the work you did during this lesson? If your observer doesn't have that background information, how can you provide it?
- Have you drawn attention to the high points in the lesson that you would like to be certain that the observer noticed?

☐ **Err on the side of including too much rather than not enough.**

☐ **Read it through and give it a final polish.**
- Did you give the document one last start-to-finish read-through for logic and for errors?
- Have you addressed any notes from your observer?
- Have you double-checked the rubrics?
- Have you asked a trusted friend to read this over? If so, have you considered this reader's feedback and addressed issues raised?

☐ **Know when to be finished. Once you've given this document your best effort, your work is complete. It's OK to set it aside and relax.**

Finding Your Voice: Your Postobservation Conference as Collaboration

A few days after my observation, I meet my evaluator in her office. She greets me warmly and tells me how much she loved seeing my students work. We talk about the strengths and what I've done to extend the students' understanding of how to use their notes as textual evidence. She offers a few suggestions on what might work, but not with an air of certainty—merely as other strategies to try because they have worked before. I provide a stack of artifacts—copies of the students' reflections from that day's lesson, the missions given to each student (paired to each student's unique needs), and the facilitation grid I used to track their participation in both this seminar and the last one these students did. I point to evidence of how each student showed growth using the grid and we talk about the students' insights. We discuss decisions I had noted in preobservation artifacts. I share reflections I had written on my lesson plans from the week before, noting how I'd address student confusion to a previous assignment. When I leave the meeting, I feel confident and energized to get back to work.

This is not a fairy tale; I had this conference. This administrator had a view of evaluation as a means to improve student learning and a way to give strong educators another way to think about their practice. Of course, I've had other postobservation conferences that were perfunctory, or that felt judgmental, or where I spent a lot of time explaining the content of the lesson so that the observer understood the pedagogy. Those kinds of conversations often show that the administrator has a deficit model in mind—a belief that the administrator needs to fix the teacher, a belief that presumes ineptness at best and negligence or malice at worst.

It's not uncommon for teachers to head into postobservation conferences with the expectation that they are there to be judged by the observer. If the judgment is favorable, the teacher may feel affirmed. If the judgment is not favorable, the teacher may feel defensive or even defective. But, no matter what the outcome, when a teacher walks into a postobservation conference expecting a judgment, both the teacher and the observer are missing out on a valuable opportunity to learn and improve.

In this chapter, we'll consider how you can reframe your conference as a dialogue with another educator and a chance to consider your classroom in another way. When you approach the conference as a collaborative effort, you can provide context for what the observer saw and help him or her to reframe what he or she thought he or she saw. This chapter offers strategies for recontextualizing what the observer noted, for providing evidence to refute points of disagreement, for using the evaluation to celebrate successes, and for creating a map of where to go next.

Just Before the Postobservation Conference: Make Final Preparations

With the preparation work you did in Chapter 8, you're already well positioned to discuss the observation. Before going into the conference, look over the responses you recorded on Professional Journal Page 8.03 to keep your strengths in mind. As you review your strengths, consider what messages about the observation you want to convey. Then, consider how you'll answer predictable questions such as, "How do you think that went?" and "Did you meet the goals you set out for the students?" Keep your answers quick and focused on the positive. Make sure you can use the language of the rubric to connect what you did with what the evaluator is looking for.

Consider how you will acknowledge anything that didn't go well, how you addressed it in the moment, and how it has helped you to grow. When discussing your choices, plan to clarify what ideas you considered and why you didn't make certain choices. Saying, "After reflecting on it last night . . . ," or "After analyzing the students' work, I think I could have . . . ," shows the observer that you are thoughtful and reflective about your work. In these responses, and in the entire conference, your goal is not to be perfect but to show growth for yourself and your students. Showing that you were aware of what was happening in your

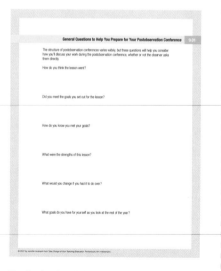

9.01

See Professional Journal Page 9.01 at the end of this chapter for a list of general questions that may help you to prepare for the postobservation conference.

(Also available online as a digital download.)

classroom and that you recognize ways to make changes demonstrates your expertise and professionalism.

If the observer has given you her or his written feedback prior to the conference, read through it carefully. See the suggestions under the heading "After the Conference: Analyze the Notes from the Observer" on page 131 for ideas about what to look for in the documentation.

When it's time for your conference, bring a pen, a notebook, and your preobservation artifacts, including your lesson plan. Also take any artifacts you prepared in Chapter 8, and if you are required to, upload them before the conference.

During the Conference: Listen and Respond

As you walk into the postobservation conference, remember: the conference is collaborative. Keep the messages that you want to share about the observation in mind. This is where knowing your students well and having great preobservation and postobservation documents and artifacts will help: you can refer to those in your comments. Take your time during the discussion. The purpose of this conversation is to use it as a way to grow, and it's much harder to do that when you are flustered.

Take Notes

Jot down notes on everything you are told. It's easy to forget the exact language later or to focus on one thing that was said and overlook other important points, and you want to have a complete picture of what was discussed. As you are taking notes, mark places where you want to respond, either in the meeting or in writing afterward.

Listen to Constructive Criticism Actively

At some point in the conversation, the observer will likely mention areas for potential improvement. When receiving this feedback, use this opportunity to ask for specifics. Try responses such as these:

- "I'd love to try your suggestion. Could you offer some specifics on how you would implement that?"

- "It's important to me that I improve. Could you give me some examples?"

- "I'd really like to meet your expectations on this, but I'm just not clear on what you're suggesting. Could you rephrase that?"

- "I want to do well and help my students. Could you tell me what you would have liked to see?"

- "It is really important to me that I do the best I can for my students, and I thought I had met the rubric expectations. Could you explain what you would have needed to see for me to be scored distinguished/proficient?"

Using this language shows that you are invested in what happens in your classroom and allows your observer to give you feedback as an expert. Just write down the observer's response for now (clarify if you need to: "I'm hearing you say X. Is that right?"). You don't necessarily need to agree, but to respond to the observation, you need specifics on what the observer is looking for, especially if you need to create a plan to show improvement. We don't expect students to grow unless we give them specific feedback. We should expect the same from our administrators.

If You Don't Think a Score Is Accurate, Ask for a Change

Don't be afraid to ask the evaluator to consider changing a score. Many teachers I spoke with when researching this book reported that they'd been successful at least some of the time in getting a score changed through evidence presented in the postobservation conference discussion.

Several teachers explained that when they don't agree with a score, they ask observers what they didn't see that they were looking for. Some said that they use the language of the rubric and back up their argument with knowledge of their students and evidence such as formative assessments. One teacher told me: "First, I ask them what was missing that would have made it the higher score. I make them explain the score to me and then I provide documentation. If they miss stuff, I provide the documentation of why it was a 4. In one case, I even offered to have students come in and explain the concept [when an observer didn't think a student understood]." Having the person doing the evaluation explain how he or she is interpreting the rubric is a key step in overcoming objections and clarifying your position.

Framing the request in a way that is nonconfrontational and shows you are seeking information as much as offering it helps the conversation feel more like a discussion than an argument. For example, if I had scored myself a 4 in an area and my observer didn't feel the same, I might say, "I'm curious as to why this is not a 4. When I look at the rubric, I'm seeing it says I needed to include X [give specifics from the rubric]. In the class you observed, we/I did Y [show clear evidence and connection to the language of the rubric]. That seems to align with the 4, don't you agree?" You can also offer artifacts or evidence to back up your belief.

Opening up a discussion about changing a score might feel unusual if you're used to considering the postobservation conference as a judgment. However, if the conference is truly a collaborative conversation, it won't be effective without your input. Questioning a score and providing evidence gives you an opportunity to help the observer to see your practice more clearly, and it gives the observer an opportunity to articulate his or her expectations more completely. Think about the way you prefer students to approach you to get more information about a grade they earned, and approach your conversation that way. Listen carefully to the response and don't become adversarial. Take notes.

Don't Discount Positive Feedback

While it is easy to focus on the negatives, make a point of taking notes about what is going well. If your observer does not offer comments on your observed strengths, ask about them. Often, we are so overwhelmed with all we do in a single class period that it's hard to give ourselves credit for the things we get right. Taking time to appreciate all that you are doing right gives your observer the opportunity to name what you're doing right as well.

After the Conference: Analyze the Notes from the Observer

If the observer provides written notes ahead of the postobservation conference, use them to do this step before the conference. If, however, you don't receive anything in writing until after the postobservation conference, follow these steps at that point. It helps to make a copy of the observer's notes or the written observation so you can mark up the text.

Assess the Notes' Accuracy

Do the written notes accurately reflect what happened during the observation and (if applicable) the postobservation conference? For example, if you already had your postobservation conference and you received all positive feedback but there are scores that are below passing, make an appointment to meet with the observer again to discuss the discrepancy. As in the conference, approach this meeting as a collaborative effort. You might start with something like: "When we met the other day, you had glowing things to say about my lesson and called it a 'model lesson,' so I'm confused by the below-satisfactory scores on some sections." Some of the scoring software is sensitive, and mistakes happen, so approach it as if it is probably an oversight and give the observer the benefit of the doubt.

Look for Assumptions and Misunderstandings

Go through carefully and look for words that are subjective; the goal of most current teacher evaluation systems is to make the process objective. For example, "Students were bored" is not objective. "Students doodled while the teacher read aloud," is objective, and it also opens the door for you to reframe the comment. Perhaps the observer concluded that the doodling students were bored. However, you might have taught your students how to sketchnote and asked them in the past to create visual representations of what they were hearing as part of your classroom procedures.

Compare the notes the observer typed up with your own notes. I've found innocent mistakes where an observer misheard a comment or left out a piece of evidence that came up in our postobservation conference but didn't end up in the evaluation. Ask the observer to change or insert such things.

Check the Document Against the Scoring Rubric

While you are going through the evidence, look back at the rubric. Sometimes evidence ends up in a different section of the written document, or it applies to more than one element of the observation. So while a student discussion may be part of your rapport with students, it is also part of questioning and discussion. Look for places where evidence was overlooked, especially if you included it in your preobservation and postobservation conference artifacts. Sometimes observers write up a draft before looking at the artifacts. Make an appointment to address any discrepancies with your observer before signing the final document.

After the Conference: Respond to the Observation Documentation

In the next chapter, we'll consider how you can use the feedback in the evaluation documentation to shape your personal development plans in the coming months and years. For now, the first order of business is to respond to the documentation from this observation.

Always write a response to your evaluator. If you are happy with the evaluation, you need only respond with a quick note, such as "Thank you for visiting my class." If something you did isn't mentioned in the evaluation itself, add it in your response:

"I'm so glad you had the opportunity to see my students preparing for the physics competition. My classes loved having the chance to compete against each other and apply what they learned to real-world problems. I hope I can hold the competition again next year and you'll be able to see their results."

However, if you have scores you feel do not accurately reflect what happened in your classroom, you need to address it. This includes scores that label your work as merely proficient when you have evidence that indicates your work is exemplary. When we let exemplary work go unnoticed, we don't just downplay own accomplishments. We also unwittingly contribute to school-wide, district-wide, and even nationwide negative perceptions of our profession.

Sharing Evaluations

I have taken my evaluation and, sight unseen, tossed it in the copier and shared it with local union representatives and fieldwork students. Many other teachers in my district also share their evaluations with the union, some choosing to redact their identifying information first. My local union, as many do, keeps an anonymous database of our evaluations that only the committee working on evaluations sees. The committee finds patterns of areas that the district administration may be focusing on or sometimes areas of disagreement in scoring. We also use this information to bring in professional development from the state level to address areas of concern or areas for growth so that members can get additional opportunities to learn new strategies.

When You Do Not Agree with a Score: Address Your Concerns

If you feel that your score does not accurately reflect your work, you can take steps to address this issue in several ways.

You might be wondering if this is worth doing. Has anyone ever seen positive results from addressing concerns about scores with observers? The answer is yes.

Many teachers I spoke with described how they had been successful in having scores changed based on conversations. There is no guarantee that you'll get the changes you're asking for, but there won't be any changes if you don't make the attempt.

Talk to the Observer

If possible, your first step should be to address your concerns face-to-face with your observer. If the observer gives you the scores before or during the postobservation conference, you can discuss the scores during that conversation. If you see an issue, use the methods described earlier in the chapter: ask for clarification, raise questions, offer evidence of your strong work in your conversation, and request a change in score. If you do not receive scores until after your conference with your observer and you find that you have concerns about the scores, schedule a time with the observer for a follow-up meeting. This need not be confrontational. If you approach the follow-up meeting with the mind-set of seeking clarification and finding a collaborative solution, most administrators will be open to this discussion.

Get Help if Necessary

If you belong to a union and are facing a serious challenge, such as a low score or an unresponsive administrator, seek out your association representative for assistance. The union has staff who are trained to respond. Do not be afraid to ask for help. Too often, teachers wait to ask for help because they are ashamed or think they can handle it on their own, and by the time they do seek help, their jobs are in jeopardy. I have seen a teacher receive a nonrenewal letter because the teacher hadn't responded to nonpassing scores on observations. Instead of reaching out to the union rep immediately after receiving poor observation scores, the teacher was silent. The administration interpreted the teacher's lack of response as a lack of professional enthusiasm. Contrary to what some believe, unions are not notified about teachers' scores on observations or evaluations. It is up to us to reach out to our reps when we need their help.

If you do not belong to a union, find a trusted mentor to help you with your response.

Respond in Writing if Necessary

Most current evaluation models allow teachers to respond in writing. If conversations do not solve the issue, you'll need to write a response to the observation documents that addresses your concerns. This is imperative if you have any scores that are below proficient. Not responding may send a message that you aren't concerned about the quality of your teaching. Be mindful of time lines for responding to evaluations and double-check them as soon as you get your evaluation. Nothing is worse than thinking you had ten business days and discovering you only had ten calendar days. While you may be angry, sarcasm (yes, even if it's very witty) and indignant language will not help you in this process. Wait until you are calm to begin working on your response. (Feel free, however, to write as angry a response as you'd like so you can vent; just throw that one away and write an objective one to actually submit.)

Use the notes you took and the rubric to go through each section. If you have previously been praised for something, especially in writing, include it in your response: "Both Mr. Jones and Mrs. Garcia found my lessons on factoring polynomials 'engaging' and 'easy to follow' in the last two years." Use objective language and stick to the facts, citing evidence and artifacts and aligning them with the rubric. Explain extenuating circumstances without making excuses. For example, instead of saying how a particular issue has never happened before, give specifics that explain the situation and that show the steps you took to benefit your students: "While J.C.'s angry outburst was uncharacteristic of him, I learned when I followed up with his mother afterward that his father recently moved out and she has been seeking help for J.C. to handle his emotions." Go through each section of the observation and respond, offering evidence to support your position. Acknowledge the areas where you received positive scores, too, adding evidence such as "The highly effective score in questioning techniques reflects the effort put into finding new ways to engage students, and I have taken two online seminars and attended a workshop to deepen my understanding of how to use these tools to best help students learn." These comments prevent the response from focusing too much on the negative and help you frame yourself as a professional who puts time into learning how to excel.

When you are through, share your draft with your union representative or a trusted mentor. Listen to your reader's ideas about how you are framing what happened. Review your response carefully for tone and strive to sound matter-of-fact rather than emotional. Stick to the facts rather than opinions or interpretations. If you can put the evaluation aside for a few days to get some emotional distance, do so.

Before submitting, read the piece aloud to yourself and double-check spelling and punctuation. This will become part of your permanent file, and presenting yourself as a competent professional is essential.

Keep Students First

In this chapter, I've discussed ways to help observers see your strengths as well as ways to address disheartening observation outcomes. This point in the evaluation process puts you and your work on prominent display. When we engage in the process as a collaborative effort, we have the opportunity to do even better work with our students in the future. However, if we let the process become a distraction from the real heart of our work—our students—our jobs can begin to feel inauthentic and empty. We didn't become teachers to argue about how well we do our job. We became teachers to teach students.

As part of your final processing of the observation, let yourself memorialize what you are doing right for your students. Make a brag sheet and put it under your desk blotter. Jot down warm comments from students and colleagues and keep them somewhere you can look at them throughout the day to remind yourself of how you are helping your students. Keep a file of positive notes from students and parents for those days when it feels like nothing is going right. And focus on your students: students are big mirrors—you get back the energy you put forth. If you exude negativity, you will get negativity. If you are cheerful and focused on the positive, it will be a lot easier to get students to join you in that energy.

The structure of postobservation conferences varies widely, but these questions will help you consider how you'll discuss your work during the postobservation conference, whether or not the observer asks them directly.

How do you think the lesson went?

Did you meet the goals you set out for the lesson?

How do you know you met your goals?

What were the strengths of this lesson?

What would you change if you had it to do over?

What goals do you have for yourself as you look at the rest of the year?

Adjusting Your Action Plan and Preparing for Unannounced Evaluations

Early in my teaching career, I was summoned to the principal's office one day without warning. I had no idea what it could have been for and my hands were clammy on the way down the stairs. After all, no one wants to be called to the principal's office. It was my first year in a new school, and the principal didn't spend much time among his staff. Faculty meetings were perfunctory affairs and we were usually dismissed after a few minutes. I had never spoken to him; he was handling a fight the day I interviewed for the position.

When I got to his office, his secretary handed me a stapled packet of papers and asked for my signature. I flipped through, unsure of what to say. It was a copy of an observation report, presumably of a lesson I had taught about nouns. I had not taught a lesson about nouns. No one had visited my classroom. The secretary smiled at me kindly. The score was good—no deficiencies. I smiled back as I signed the paper. "When did he come see me?" I asked.

"Oh, he watched you through your classroom window," the secretary replied.

To this day, I have no idea if the principal had ever been outside my window watching me teach. Even if he had, how could he possibly have learned everything he needed to know about my work while peeking through a small window and listening through a closed door? I approached my union representative about the evaluation. He assured me that I did what I needed to do in signing it and that, in his opinion, it was best not to say anything. I went back to my classroom wondering what was expected of me during an actual observation and what was expected of me as a teacher.

I wish I could say that this kind of situation is unusual. Unfortunately, my own experience and the experiences of teachers I've spoken with about their own unannounced observations show that surreal circumstances like these are not uncommon: One teacher was visited by multiple evaluators on back-to-back days. Another was observed on the day before final exams and was criticized for not introducing new material. Once an observer watched a classroom while standing in the flower bed outside (which, understandably, did not go unnoticed by the students, who then found it hard to stay focused) and then told the teacher his class was off task and distracted. Another observer showed up late and left early. Rather than simply accepting this as normal, as I did when I was a new teacher, we can find ways to take charge of and shape the narrative of these observations.

An essential component of today's teacher evaluations is our growth as educators. In this chapter, we'll use the feedback from your evaluation to consider next steps. We'll revisit the areas for growth that you identified in Chapter 2, reassess the action plan you developed in Chapter 3, and consider how we might target more specific areas for growth in the remainder of the year. This prepares you for unannounced observations, yes, but it also has the potential to help you improve the work you're doing with and for your students.

A side effect of today's evaluation systems is that we must also be proficient in *showing* how we grow as educators. This chapter offers targeted strategies for building in opportunities for dynamic lessons within the remaining units of instruction. Lessons such as these will demonstrate how both you and your students are improving and learning, whether you are evaluated by the same observer or not, and whether you know when the next observation is coming or not.

Adjusting Your Course

Now that you have feedback from the observation, you can consider if and how to adjust your action plan for the year. Refer to the following:

- the notes you made at the beginning of the year about areas in which you wanted to grow (Professional Journal Pages 2.01 and 2.03)

- the notes you took during the postobservation conference

- the official documentation of the observation

10.01

See Professional Journal Page 10.01 at the end of this chapter for a reproducible note-taking page on areas for growth.

(Also available online as a digital download.)

Look at potential areas for growth noted in these documents. Remember that a growth area does not necessarily reflect a weakness—it is a place for you to learn more. Now, consider which areas of growth to prioritize. Where will you concentrate your efforts before your next observation or your year-end evaluation? Why? If you have sections of your evaluation that scored below passing, focus on those first. If your overall evaluation is strong, look first at anything your evaluator suggested as growth areas. Or perhaps there's a comment that asks you to "continue to . . ." and then lists things you are already doing. This provides a door for you to do some research and delve deeper. For example, when I work with students one-on-one, I might decide I'd like to learn more about making conferring even more focused on something that students can use to move forward immediately.

See Professional Journal Page 10.02 at the end of this chapter for a reproducible planning page.

(Also available online as a digital download.)

Planning for Growth

Take time to think through what you'd like to work on, and then brainstorm ways you could gather more information on that subject and begin making a plan. You may also want to look back at the notes you made on Professional Journal Pages 3.02 and 3.03. Using my previous example, I might read a book about coaching conferences with students, find blog posts on the topic, or seek out other educators I know to get their suggestions. In an ideal situation, I'd find someone who is using conferring effectively and watch him or her. In some districts, visiting the classrooms of other professionals to see strategies being implemented well is part of the culture. If it isn't something that happens in your school, perhaps ask a colleague you know is successful with a particular strategy if you can stop by and listen in for a few minutes.

Once I've researched, I can break down what I've discovered into clear, manageable steps for myself. I might determine that I'm going to focus just on reading conferences, for example. I might create a sheet to take notes during the conferences to help me gather information about the questions I ask and the responses I get. I might make a list of a few questions to begin with until I am comfortable with those questions and how to probe further. Once I've mastered those questions, I can add to my repertoire. After I work with students, I can reflect on the effectiveness of the strategies and determine next steps for myself, including these activities in my lesson plans to show that I'm doing these things. I might even videotape myself conferring (even if I don't show it to anyone else) to look more objectively at how I'm working with a student. These changes might not be big, but they are purposeful. If I keep asking myself, "What do I know about student learning? How do I know it? How do I know that's an effective measurement?" I'll always come back to ways to improve my efforts for my students. Also, all of this work provides artifacts that show the connection between what I am learning and how it impacts student learning.

Communicating Your Growth

As you are considering the changes you'll be making in the coming weeks and months, also consider how you'll let observers or administrators know about the work you're doing. Of course, if you are working on improving your practice and have subsequent observations ahead, plan on discussing what you are doing during those observation conferences. However, if you attend a great workshop or a webinar, don't be afraid to send your administrators an email letting them know that you are engaging in these activities. (If you are doing a lot of them, sending an email once a month is probably sufficient.) Letting them know what you're doing and how it's valuable in your classroom is a great way to make sure your administration knows what you are working on. A quick note is all you need to write: "This weekend, I attended this conference and heard some great information. I'll be trying out X in my classroom this semester to see if students connect better with the material." You might even want to share what you learned with your colleagues (which is also worth documenting, whether you send them an email, put a copy of a blog post that you thought they could use in their mailboxes, or are asked to present at a department meeting or inservice). While most of this will be in your end-of-the-year portfolio or come up at your summative evaluation conference, keeping your administrators informed means that they have a better idea of the work you have been doing all along. You might want to put a copy of your emails (and any responses you get back!) in your professional development journal, especially because things come up and sometimes a different evaluator will handle your end-of-the-year evaluation.

Ensuring There's Time Between Observations

Keep in mind that your district and state policy may vary on subsequent evaluations. I was once evaluated by two different administrators in the same class on back-to-back days before I had even had a chance to discuss my teaching with the first administrator. In some places, this is fair game. In others, a set amount of time or the first observation cycle must be complete before subsequent evaluations may take place. I once had an administrator show up to my class, and when I said, "What a nice surprise! Ms. X was here a few days ago," that administrator said there had been a mix-up in the schedule and excused herself so she could visit someone else. Miscommunication happens, so if you think it is too soon to be observed, politely let the subsequent observer know if you were visited recently or haven't received the previous observer's evaluation yet.

Planning for Future (and Likely Unannounced) Observations

If you have another announced observation scheduled, the process you used for the previous observation (outlined in Chapters 6–9) will be your guide again. This time, however, be sure to take the feedback from the previous observation into account as you plan your observation lesson.

To prepare for unannounced observations, be ready to show the things your evaluation model requires to an observer. This means that these areas need to become part of your everyday practice. Consider how to best show growth from what the observer has already seen in your classroom—both developing your strengths and remediating perceived weaknesses. Whether you agree with your administrators' scoring or not, set yourself up for success by adding to your repertoire in that area or delving deeper into how you use that strategy. If one of the things you needed or wanted to strengthen was connecting to previous learning, for example, create an anchor chart that hangs on the wall throughout the unit that you or students update regularly to show that you took the suggestion seriously and implemented a strategy to make it visible to students and outside observers. If you were going to work on pacing, take a few moments to sketch out how much time you need for each section of your lesson and use a timer to stay on track. If you were going to improve monitoring student learning, jot down a few quick formative assessment strategies you can use throughout the lesson. Whatever growth you want to show from your previous observation, prepare materials to address that in a visible way when someone comes in.

The classroom walls can also help to show growth: Displays of student work can demonstrate the journey you've been on together since the previous observation. A bulletin board that shows you gathered more information about student needs or anchor charts that show students are working with information in manageable chunks can help make your case.

Of course, your growth as an educator isn't limited to what observers see. When you've made shifts that are in your students' best interest, incorporating them into your repertoire and using them frequently (even when you're not expecting to be observed), your students will benefit and you will help yourself to use your new tools and skills more naturally.

Addressing Weak Scores

Being told your teaching falls below expectations is always hard to hear. However, under the teacher evaluation models that require standardized rubrics to score your teaching, addressing areas of perceived weakness, whether valid or not, is key. Your personal growth plan needs to show what you did to learn something new, how you applied it, and how you know what effect it had on student learning. For example, if your score in *questioning* was marked as below proficient, create a folder that shows how you addressed this. You might show that you completed an online webinar, attended a workshop, or read and reflected on blog posts about ways to improve your questioning technique. Put your notes and reflections from those activities in the folder. You might also create protocols to teach students how to ask good questions and put the handouts from that in the folder, along with photos of your whiteboard and any anchor charts you made to help students (and yourself) stay focused on the kinds of questions you wanted to ask. You might post the essential question in a highly visible location and refer to it while you teach and then have students periodically reflect on the essential question, adding what new information they have learned to their answer. You might help students engage in Socratic seminars and literature circles. You might have students reflect on their own growth, as well, letting them define strong questions and asking them how a great question helps them think about things differently. You could keep sample artifacts of student work and reflections, as well as reflections of your own about how the lesson went, what you would do differently next time, and what your next steps need to be.

In some cases, you might be given an action plan by your administration that dictates tasks you should undertake to remediate your skills. If so, make sure that you are not only completing everything by the deadline but exceeding the minimum requirements set forth so that you can show your interest in improving. Be proactive and seek out additional resources and opportunities that extend what you were asked to do. Keep notes, reflections, lesson plans, handouts, and student work samples as appropriate to show that you are applying what you are doing to your classroom.

Practice the strategy or element you've been asked to improve so that you have both evidence of working on it over time and your reflections on how you are implementing it. Gaining comfort and facility at using the element or strategy will allow you to demonstrate it fluidly during a follow-up observation.

Keep Students First

As you reflect on your progress, both personally and through someone else's eyes in an observation, your key question should be on what helps students most. Think about your next observation and consider what you want to show that your students are able to do. What can they do now with help that they could learn to do independently? How do you know students are learning? What haven't they learned yet that they will be able to do with scaffolding or benchmark lessons? This chapter has discussed how you can plan and demonstrate growth, but the purpose for that growth is, as always, your drive to do your best by your students. It's also a lifeline for you: keeping your students at the forefront of your practice keeps you energized to teach them more than any evaluation score could.

Use this page to consider all of your potential areas for growth. Then circle the two or three areas you'll focus on most directly before your next observation or your year-end evaluation.

Areas of Growth That I Identified Early in the Year:

Areas of Growth Suggested by My Most Recent Observation:

Area in Which I Plan to Grow: _____

I am targeting this area because (check all that apply):

☐ it will help my students

☐ it interests me

☐ a student has expressed a need for it

☐ an observer or supervisor has named it as an area of focus for me

☐ other:

What My Practice Will Look Like in This Area:	What My Practice Currently Looks Like in This Area:

Resources I'll Use to Grow (check all that apply):

☐ professional reading (list specific titles)

☐ in-person or interactive online professional development (list specific events)

☐ coaching from _____ (explain how you'll work with this coach)

☐ mentoring from _____ (explain your plan for how you'll work with this mentor)

☐ my own action research (explain your process)

☐ other:

What I Will Share with Observers and/or Supervisors (check all that apply):

☐ updates about my professional learning (events attended, books read, etc.)

☐ ideas worth sharing that I've learned from reading, mentors, and professional development

☐ student artifacts from my classroom that show the benefits of my growth

☐ other:

Reflecting Throughout the Year

One year, after I assigned yet another reflection following an assignment, a student lost her composure and started yelling. "Another reflection? Why do I have to reflect? What is this 'thinking theory' you have? No one in the world thinks about things all the time!" Several years later, she visited my classroom while on college break. "That thinking theory you had? I just want you to know, you're onto something there. College expects me to think. A lot." I'm still in touch with that student, and we still laugh about my "thinking theory" and about her insistence that no one else thinks. While I am sure she was asked to think in her other classes, my class was probably the first where the act of reflection was presented explicitly as a way of learning.

Many teaching evaluation models require reflection. While we can likely meet at least the evaluation's bare requirements of reflection by documenting our work over the year, we're more likely to benefit from reflection if we embrace it as a truly useful tool. In *How We Think*, John Dewey (1910) writes that true reflective thought identifies a course of action, a next step to improve. Merely thinking about how we know something to be true isn't enough; we need to use that to determine the path forward. Further, Dewey reminds us that reflective thought also requires us to approach our thinking with "hesitation [and] doubt" while also actively seeking new evidence (8), and that it requires us to suspend our judgment until we can gather more information (9). For our purposes, then, reflection means taking time to consider what we know about ourselves, our students, and our practice, and how we know those things to be true. The answers to these questions provide a foundation for our future decisions on how to proceed, whether that is in structuring a unit, designing an assessment, or building a relationship with a student. In her interpretation of Dewey's ideas on reflective thinking, researcher and professor Carol Rodgers (2002) reminds us that among the key aspects of Dewey's assertions on reflection is the commitment to giving fair consideration to all possibilities and the willingness to change if that's what is required to move ahead. Reflective thinking is, then, having an openness to consider other ideas and the courage to change our practice based on the evidence we find. This chapter includes ideas for creating opportunities for reflection, with forms to help you spot patterns, see breakthroughs, and correct the course you planned earlier in the year.

Make Reflection a Daily Habit

Building a habit of reflection pays off not only in your evaluation (because you'll be prepared to discuss your decision making) but in other ways as well. Planning becomes easier because you have taken the time to think through what has and hasn't worked and what you need to do next. Basing decisions on evidence makes you a more confident teacher, and students are likely to trust you if you can answer their "why" questions beyond "Because it's in the curriculum." Learning to reflect daily will help your teaching and your sanity.

Fine-Tune Your Work for Next Time

Leave your written plans and classroom assignments on your desk and jot down notes at the end of a class period or the end of the day: Where do you need to adjust this lesson next time you teach it? What adjustments will you need to make in upcoming lessons to make sure students are ready and appropriately challenged?

Think of Every Assignment as a Clue

Take a moment after you've graded your students' work and consider what you can learn from the responses. Use an informal formative assessment, whether a thumbs-up/thumbs-down check or a sheet of paper for students to tell you what they thought was difficult about the test or what part of the lesson they think they're most likely to forget how to do.

Add Artifacts to Your Portfolio

Continually look for artifacts to include in your portfolio. I photograph every bulletin board right after it goes up. I put the revised test or rubric or set of project directions into my professional development journal when I make copies for students. I use a folder labeled "Copy" to collect student work samples as they are submitted. The next time I head to the faculty room, I run off copies for my records.

As you choose work to include, consider showcasing not just exemplary work but the work that shows what most students produced or that indicates a need for intervention, whether it's work on following directions, a reminder to the student and parents about the importance of attendance, or scheduling an extra help session for that student.

Focus on Individual Students

I had a student who suddenly became confrontational and frustrated whenever I gave him directions. Rather than ignoring this behavior, I called his mother. She said that she was out of work and didn't think her fifteen-year-old son knew, but they were on the verge of losing their home. Because I'd focused on his needs, I was able to solve the problem in my class, get the family in touch with resources to help, give the parent a way into the difficult conversation she needed to have with her son, and refer the student to a counselor.

Find a Simple System That Works for You

I use penciled-in notes on my written plans for the week, which I leave out on my desk so I can write reflective comments as soon as I think of them, and sticky notes of ideas I have when I look over student work. There's usually a sticky note of common errors in papers I'm marking, which becomes a guide for me going forward. Your own system might be completely different. What's important is that you find a way to make reflection a sustainable habit for you.

Reflect with Your Students

I always share the reflecting I do with my students. This allows me to model reflection and opens a dialogue that goes beyond the personal reflections they write. Sharing my thinking about what I'm doing and why I'm making a change shows that adults make changes when needed and allows students a voice in the decisions that I'm making.

Ask Students to Reflect in Writing

My students regularly write reflections after assignments. Persuasive essay? Students write a reflection on how they can tell they were writing an argument and not an analysis. Project work? Students write about how they interacted with their group and about their own contributions. Quiz? Students jot down how they studied and how they could study more effectively next time. At the end of the quarter, students write reflections that include how they know they have grown as readers and what evidence they can use to support their thinking. I give students forms, essays, questionnaires, and blank half sheets of paper to capture their thinking about the process of learning as much as the products they've created.

Invite Students into Problem Solving

When students struggle, I step back and have them reflect and then we work together to make a new plan. I sometimes have students create a new anchor chart or annotate one that we made earlier. We might take new notes, look at student work samples, or create a new response collectively on the board that students can copy into their notes as another model. What matters most is that I explain to my students what work I did in reflecting, in thinking about where we have been and where we are going, and, if we need to change course, make it clear what led me to think this way. The power of asking students to consider what they have learned, or why they believe they understand a concept, or how they can use new skills, lies in allowing the students' thinking to take center stage. Showing them how I think through and reflect both models the process for students and lets them know that their thinking matters because it drives my thinking and my decisions about the class.

Sometimes, depending on how much time we have (curriculum pressures being what they are), I even lay out for students what I see and what result we need and let them figure out the path forward. I occasionally hand out slips of paper and take a secret-ballot poll of what should happen next; I write the ideas on the board and keep a tally of what gets multiple votes. We then discuss any further ideas, see if we can combine suggestions, and agree on a plan. Other times, we just brainstorm ideas and then take a vote. Letting students discuss ideas in small groups and report out to the class allows everyone a voice in what happens in the classroom, and it allows me to ask them how they arrived at their answers, why they think their strategy will work, and how much time they need. Allowing students to create a plan and evaluate it helps them learn how to plan. Empowering students through reflective practice helps them see their learning as their responsibility and not just mine.

Schedule Time for Reflection

The beginning of the year is always so hectic. I don't know about you, but I feel like by the time I pick up my head and look around, it's the middle of October if I'm lucky. I start off with the best of intentions to record more of my reflections, but somehow I get off track. Using the planning calendar, I now schedule in some time to write reflections, not only for my evaluation artifacts but because research shows that written reflection is effective in helping us think systematically about our teaching.

On my calendar, I jot down the word *reflect* on the days *after* progress reports and report cards are due. At those moments, I know I'll have a snapshot of how students are doing, making it an optimum time to reflect on the big questions rather than just the quick daily reflections that are unconnected to larger learning goals. In addition, I have students write reflections at those points, so I can compare how students perceive their progress with my evaluations.

Here are some questions that help me reflect at the midpoint and end of a grading segment:

See Professional Journal Page 11.01 at the end of this chapter for a reproducible reflection form.

(Also available online as a digital download.)

- ***How am I feeling?*** This question lets me take my own pulse. Do I feel rushed? Relaxed? Self-care matters, and sometimes I forget to stop and think about how I feel. There are days when I stop to think about how I am feeling and discover I have a strong headache that I was too busy to notice. By the midpoints and ends of quarters, this can be compounded.

- ***How are my students feeling?*** I can also look at my students for clues about how *they're* feeling. Are they comfortable? Tense? Engaged? Distant? And, of course, I can always ask them directly in conversations or even inventories or questionnaires. Often, I use their bell-work time to wander around the room and engage them in conversation. "How are you? How did you do on last night's assignment? What do you think of the book?" During independent reading and readers and writers workshop, I have a lot of these conversations, but I work to gather this information regularly for planning and to know my students better.

- ***What skills or content do I need to adjust my planning for over the next few weeks?*** I take a moment to flip through the online grade book and compare what I'm doing with the curriculum map I made for the year and the more detailed map with exact lesson plans. Are students making progress quicker that I had planned?

Do they need more time with something than I'd originally thought? Where am I headed, and do I need to change my route to get there?

- *What activities have gone well? Which could be improved or replaced?* Here, I consider the students' experiences as well as my own goals— maybe they *do* understand sonnets better after a particular writing activity, but if they were miserable during the exercise, perhaps I could find a better way to address that topic. What have I learned recently that might help these students? What outside resources (a video clip, advertisement, article) have I come across that would help students understand this unit better the next time I teach it or will make a bridge to connect understanding to a later unit? What activities that I love have I been overrelying upon? I look for ways to address the needs of the students I have as well as consider what to change for future students.

- *What procedures have been useful and productive? Which need more practice or need to be reconsidered?* Again, I take students' experiences into account here. Are the procedures genuinely helpful to students? Sometimes I ask them how we could streamline procedures to make things easier—could we move a marker bin to a more convenient location, alter how we submit online documents, or give students more ownership of a task? For example, after students said I always put off returning papers until after a lesson and ran out of time, I changed the procedure: now I put the papers in a rack and students hand them out as soon as they get to class because they are eager to see the comments.

- *What formative assessments have I used that have given me useful feedback?* How have I been collecting evidence of student learning? Am I relying on one method too much? What might work as well or better? For formative assessments, I need to think about what I want to know, how I'm going to use that information, and what is the best way to get that information.

- *How well has my teaching (considering interruptions and unplanned events that have come up) matched the plan I made for the year (see Chapter 4)?* What should I consider changing next year? These are big-picture questions that let me think about the sequence of lessons, activities that I could improve or replace, new ideas or materials I could add, and better ways to present information.

When I'm done with my reflections, I make photocopies of student work samples and reflections as well as copies of some of the lesson plans I made a lot of changes to and put them with my reflection notes so I have the artifacts and reflections together. As the year goes on, I flip through the reflections from the other quarters and pay attention to issues that arise more than once, as those might be places I need to seek out other sources of information to help me.

If your evaluation system, like mine, requires you to keep up-to-date logs of parent communications, use these scheduled reflection times to flip through your planner and notes and update those logs. If your system requires logs of professional development activities with hours, or extracurricular activities, update those during these reflection periods. Making an appointment to do it six or eight times a year, in addition to observations, means that you'll never be too far behind or overwhelmed. I use the time at the midpoint and the end of the quarter to make sure I have logged all of the emails to parents that I don't have time to log during the day (I use my email program's Sent folder, where I keep copies of all my emails).

Finally, reflection time can be a reminder to take care of yourself. Straighten up that drawer that frustrates you every day. Bring your favorite tea to work to help you relax. Schedule that massage. Flip through photos of students engaged in successful projects or memories of past school events. Make a point to catch up with that colleague you rarely run into because your schedules conflict. Buy a new box of your favorite pens so you don't go crazy looking for where you left the last one. Most important, give yourself a break. Don't stress yourself over the things you could have done better or differently. Don't feel bad about yourself because you meant to reflect daily and fell behind. Give yourself permission not to be perfect, and take a quiet moment before getting back to work.

Reevaluate the Goals on Your Plan

Once you have a plan and you have investigated the opportunities available, periodically reevaluate the personal growth plans you created in Chapter 2 (see Professional Journal Pages 2.01 and 2.03). Does the professional development plan that you mapped out in Chapter 3 still feel like a good fit, or are you seeing new directions you'd like to explore? You may want to review the professional development options listed in Chapter 3 to remind yourself of the range of available possibilities. You might add some activities that you didn't realize existed when you created the original plan. You might add others because of curricular changes or in response to observation needs.

Take a moment to analyze what you are working on. Are you choosing a mixture of what is required or expected as well as what interests you? Have you balanced learning for school with learning for yourself? While there is often overlap between what you teach and your outside interests, don't be afraid to try something new and push yourself out of your routines. Take a painting class or learn to synchronize swim. Join a genealogy group or play mahjong. Do something for yourself. If it lends itself to your classroom directly, excellent. But if you are doing it just to find your own joy of learning again, that's also important to bring to the classroom. It helps you to keep in mind what it feels like to be a learner, which helps you to see things from your students' perspectives.

It's true that many professional learning opportunities are not free, and some are even quite expensive. However, many resources are available for teachers. Don't rush to cut something from your plan before you investigate how you might get funding. Some professional associations have funding for research or attending conventions. Local nonprofit organizations may have a code or voucher for you to access professional development resources. Your local parent-teacher organization may help if you can show how your plan relates to student learning. DonorsChoose.org and personal donation sites such as GoFundMe may also help get you to your goals.

Keep Students First

Ultimately, all of our reflection is for the purpose of improving our work and meeting our students' needs. Let your students guide you: What questions do they ask that you aren't sure how to answer? What do you think they would love to know more about? What new ideas do you think they don't know about and would like to explore? What are they curious about that you could learn more about, too? Keeping students at the forefront of your decisions about what to try, what to continue doing, and what to learn will ensure you never stray too far from your goals.

How Am I Feeling?   How Are My Students Feeling?

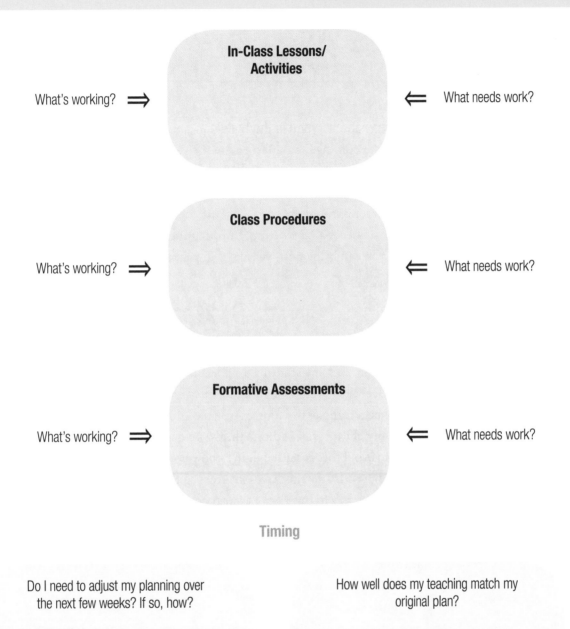

In-Class Lessons/ Activities

What's working? ⟹   ⟸ What needs work?

Class Procedures

What's working? ⟹   ⟸ What needs work?

Formative Assessments

What's working? ⟹   ⟸ What needs work?

Timing

Do I need to adjust my planning over the next few weeks? If so, how?

How well does my teaching match my original plan?

157

Celebrating Your Successes: The End-of-the-Year Evaluation

By the end of the year, everyone in the building—students and adults alike—can feel the pull of the upcoming break. The end of the year presents us with a time to celebrate our accomplishments and to put together our plan for the next year while we are still fully immersed in school life, rather than when we've had a few weeks away from the everyday realities of our jobs. This chapter is a guide for assembling evidence of your professional growth and finishing the year focused on renewal and self-care, so that you can bring positive energy to your students the next year.

Ending the Year with Students: Reflecting Together and Celebrating Accomplishments

At the end of the year, I ask my students to reflect on their growth throughout the year. We look back at their work folders, and they laugh at what they thought was good work in the beginning of the course. We take an inventory of skills, content, and attitudes. Many of them say, "I didn't think you could get me to like this, but I do," or "I used to avoid this because I didn't know how to do it, and now it feels easy." Looking at how our students have experienced the journey we have taken with them gives us another way to think about our practice. Many years, I have made notes to drop a certain unit because the students complained about it, but at the end of the year when I asked them to evaluate each unit, that was the one they asked me to keep. Sometimes we let the moment of "I don't want to do this" overwhelm the satisfaction of having done it, and we make decisions that won't allow future students to grow in the same way.

At the end of the year, I often make a video using an easy online tool such as Animoto. I type in some of the memorable comments from throughout the year and add in video clips and images of us working together. Students are always amazed at how many things we did that they have forgotten. "Remember that?" echoes through the room. We've had end-of-the-year celebrations that allowed students to work together more closely because they already knew each other, with activities

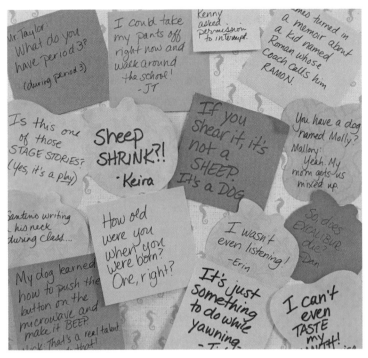

Figure 12.1 A glimpse of part of my wall of fame

such as six people walking across the room while holding beach balls between them. Other years we have had a final wrap-up class discussion of what we learned and the moments of insight that brought us there.

High school chemistry teacher Luann Christensen Lee has her students write in a Google doc anonymously, sharing "silly things" from throughout the year, what worked or didn't work for them in the class, and hints for students in class the next year ("1. Wear goggles. 2. Don't forget to wear goggles."). Luann says, "Sometimes it's more telling than what they would tell me directly because there aren't names attached."

High school special education teacher Lisa Sidorick-Weise says her end-of-the-year wrap-up for students is a celebration where they have refreshments and reflect on how much they've all grown. There's a conversation about what students thought did and didn't work for them, and students share their own milestones. "One student said, 'I never passed history before,' and that student had an A in my class," Lisa remembers.

High school Spanish teacher Aracelli Iacovelli hands out "diplomas" and little toys such as maracas or crazy glasses, recognizing the highest averages in the class and praising students individually for their achievements throughout the year.

Middle school English language arts and history teacher Keisha Rembert celebrates her students' learning with an end-of-the-year gallery walk, where she hangs up their work from throughout the year around the room. "They write letters to themselves and their parents," Rembert explains. "We look at pieces as we write the letters. Students can see where they saw themselves on the first day versus now, and the parents love getting the letters." Keisha has also had her students create videos introducing her to her students the following year—a way of wrapping up one year and carrying the energy of those students to the next year.

When the students are finished with their reflections, the real work of the year-end begins. I have a tradition of curling up with a cup of tea and reading through the reflections and then posting anonymous excerpts on Twitter to celebrate what they learned, which I can then compile using a tool such as Storify. That compilation goes into my professional reflections, and because I usually comment on how amazing I think students' ideas are, my reflections are captured along with their words.

Take time before you wrap up the year to revisit your personal growth plan, created in Chapter 2. Look over what kinds of changes you made along the way. Which items are worth moving to the summer or to next year's plan? Which are no longer relevant or worth the time and opportunity investment? Give yourself some credit for the hard work you did this year.

See Professional Journal Page 12.01 at the end of this chapter for a reproducible student reflection sheet.

(Also available online as a digital download.)

Looking Back on *Your* Year

Now for the final piece of the puzzle: just as students need to look through their year to make their final reflections, so do we. The end-of-the-year reflection is often not required by an evaluation model. However, because the work of John Dewey (1910) and Donald Schön (1983) support reflection as a key to professional growth, I'm advocating it, if for no other reason than to give ourselves credit for all that we have accomplished.

Take time to look through your documentation of the year: artifacts, reflections along the way, logs, journals, and, if you used the planner all year, the planner. Think about how you were feeling at different points in the year. How did your feelings shape your classroom experience at those times? How did your feelings shape your memory of those times? Sometimes, we are so overwhelmed by negative feelings that we don't appreciate the work we are doing.

Here are some questions to help you think about your year:

- What was your biggest challenge this year?

- What was your biggest accomplishment?

- What are you most proud of in your teaching this year?

- When you look back at the professional development you did this year, what was most valuable? How do you know? Using that knowledge, what can you do to find valuable professional development in the future?

- Where did you grow most as an educator this year? How do you know?

- What one thing would you have changed about your year? Why?

- What will you do differently next year?

- Write down your favorite memory from each of your classes this year.

- What did you not expect this year? How did you deal with it?

- How did you collaborate professionally this year? How effective was this? How do you know?

- How will you work to collaborate next year?

- Knowing what you know now, what advice would you have given yourself on the first day of school? Will it apply next year? What lesson can you take from it?

12.02

See Professional Journal Page 12.02 at the end of this chapter for reproducible journaling pages on success and growth.

(Also available online as a digital download.)

- Which students showed the most growth? How do you know?

- What strategies were most effective with students this year? How do you know?

- What lessons can you take with you from this year? What lessons can you take to your life outside the classroom?

- What brought you joy this year?

Compiling Your End-of-Year Evaluation Documentation

Most evaluators require teachers to provide some evidence of their professional growth throughout the year, as discussed when we unpacked the evaluation rubrics in Chapter 3. If you've been keeping artifacts and filling out the reproducibles in this book throughout the year, you'll be ahead on putting everything together. Use your professional development journal to populate any end-of-the-year portfolio you need to submit. Some teachers are expected to document as much of their year and their work as possible; others are asked to produce evidence of specific areas.

Make sure you include the work you did with this book because it is evidence of ongoing reflective practice, which is valued in most evaluation rubrics. For **Danielson** and **Marzano**, this is Domain 4. For **McREL**, it's Standard V. For **Stronge**, the Documentation Log requires a communication log and evidence of professional growth with a cover sheet that lists many other artifacts that teachers should collect throughout the year.

Before you meet with an evaluator about your evidence, take time to go back through and annotate, either directly on the evidence or with sticky notes, the purpose of each artifact and what standard it applies to. Include a variety of artifacts for each aspect of the professional domain.

See Professional Journal Page 12.03 at the end of this chapter for a checklist of possible types of evidence to gather.

(Also available online as a digital download.)

Show How Your Work Aligns with the Rubric

If you have been keeping up with the reflections scheduled every few weeks on your calendar, the end-of-the-year assembly is often a matter of double-checking, adding a few weeks of updates, and printing or uploading your documents. If you have fallen behind, carve out some time to work on this, especially if you are required to have a complete log with artifacts of everything. Some districts or administrative teams require only that teachers be able to access the information and do not require seeing everything assembled together. In those cases, just peruse what you have to be certain there are no glaring omissions.

Use any checklists provided by your district and in your evaluation model. Just as you did at the beginning of the year, go back through the standards and look closely at the rubrics. If the highest level of the rubric calls for you to not only reflect on your practice but also adapt your methods or teaching materials, be certain to include those adaptations. If the highest level requires you to show that students are tracking their progress, get copies of student logs. Most of the models call for examples of student work of some kind and reflection on lessons. Suggestions of what to include are at the end of this chapter. Showcase how many different things you do and how many different ways you reach students and their families.

For the **Marzano** model, keep evidence that shows you are a leader and that you help others with specific areas as defined in the rubrics. Those evaluated with the **Danielson** model or a modification of it will need to show how students initiated and maintained many of the artifacts and procedures to earn a top score. The **Stronge** model requires additional forms and paperwork be kept throughout the year as well, including student surveys.

Responding to Your Year-End Evaluation

You've made it through all your required observations, so now there's just one thing left: your end-of-the-year evaluation. The process for calculating your final score will depend on your evaluation model and your state and district policies. Different districts and states weight different domains or standards differently, and some models already account for the inclusion of test scores or other criteria such as student evaluations. Regardless, plan to bring notes on your accomplishments for the year. If you aren't required to write a formal plan for the next year, make some notes on what your goals for next year might be, such as learning a new technique, developing new ways to incorporate technology, or studying more content or pedagogy relevant to your teaching assignment.

Know Your Story

As with your postobservation conference preparations, make sure you know what story you are telling about your students, your teaching, and your school year ahead of time. How will you frame the events of the year? As overcoming challenges? As having new areas of growth and success? As integrating new partnerships with outside resources? Think about how you want to capture your year as a snapshot: What are you most proud of? How did you grow as an educator? Can your struggles be seen as opportunities for growth? Can you focus on the work you did with specific classes or students? Control the narrative you tell yourself and be positive about what you've accomplished.

Bring Evidence of Your Work to the Conference

Bring evidence of your story with you, especially if you've had observations where you've been scored below proficiency. Make sure you bring evidence not only of how you improved your own learning but of how you applied it in your classroom. Artifacts such as journal entries, notes from workshops you attended or books or articles you read, lesson plans that show your incorporation of these ideas, samples of student work (if relevant), scoring rubrics, assessments, and student reflections as well as your own will all support your presentation of yourself as a professional.

Consider Writing a Response

Writing a response is a good idea even if your final evaluation is positive. Thank the school or administration for allowing you to work with the students there. Mention the highlights of your year or your professional achievements and successes in or out of the classroom this year if they weren't included in the evaluator's comments. If the evaluation notes any weaknesses, you definitely want to respond. See Chapters 8 and 9 for suggestions on how to respond, and don't forget to include your union representative or a trusted mentor in giving you feedback before you submit your response.

Putting *Yourself* First

The other chapters in this book have ended with a reminder to keep students first. But now, at the end of the year, it's time to focus on yourself.

If possible, take time to celebrate the end of the year with colleagues. Toast another year in the books and spend some time remembering the good times of the year. Reach out to new teachers and offer support and encouragement. Jot a note of gratitude to a staff member you can always count on to help in a pinch or whose efficiency makes your job easier (perhaps a secretary, your media specialist, or a guidance counselor?). Reach out to supportive parents and thank them for their help this year. Taking a few moments to connect with others is good for us and reminds us that none of us can do this work alone.

Think about the design you created for your students' year and feel pride. Tell yourself the story of your year, and share the story of your students, your classroom, your year. What we tell ourselves about ourselves matters, but what we tell others about ourselves and our work matters, too.

Summer can be a time for deepening professional learning, for finding new concepts, strategies, and ways of seeing your classroom. You might collaborate with a like-minded teacher and find ways to create new materials or units together. You might innovate with someone who teaches a different level, a different content area, or even in a different state to bring a fresh perspective to your classroom. Perhaps this is the year that you also spend some time looking at the policies proposed in your state or at the national level and become well versed on what those proposals say and what they mean for you and the students in your classroom. We can prepare ourselves to advocate for our profession, ourselves, and our students.

Summer is also a time to remember that designing our own experiences and our own lives matters just as much. Think about the life you want to be living and do one thing that brings you closer to that, whether it's signing up for a class, starting a journal, or making plans to spend time with friends. It's easy to get caught up in the daily life of school and forget the work-life balance. Take a moment, especially if you didn't do it during the school year, to think about how to create a life you want to be living, too. You deserve to spend as much time planning your own life as you do your lessons. Part of what we offer students is not just ways to learn but examples of ways to *be* in this world. We owe it to our students to be refreshed and recharged for the start of a new year. Bring a new perspective, a new set of experiences, a new piece of yourself to your classroom next year. You've taken charge of the story of your classroom. Now make that one part of the story of your life.

12.01   **End-of-the-Year Reflection**

We made it! Before we wrap up, I'd like you to take a few minutes to think about all the learning we've shared, activities we've completed, projects we worked on, papers we wrote, and stories we read.

1.   What is your favorite memory of this class?

_____
_____
_____

2.   Which unit was your favorite? Why?

_____
_____
_____

3.   Which unit did you find most challenging?

_____
_____
_____

4.   Which activities helped you learn the most? How do you know?

_____
_____
_____

5.   Which activities will you remember ten years from now? Why?

_____
_____
_____

6.   What did you get better at doing this year? How do you know?

_____
_____
_____

7.   What surprised you most in what we studied in class? Why?

_____
_____
_____

8.   What changes should I consider for next year?

_____
_____
_____

Take a moment to remember the best parts of this year.

What was my biggest accomplishment? What am I most proud of in my work this year?

Which students showed the most growth? How do I know? What lessons and strategies were most effective?

What professional development was most valuable this year? How do I know? What brought me joy this year?

Where did I grow most this year? What is my favorite memory from each class this year?

Think about how you grew and how you want to grow next year.

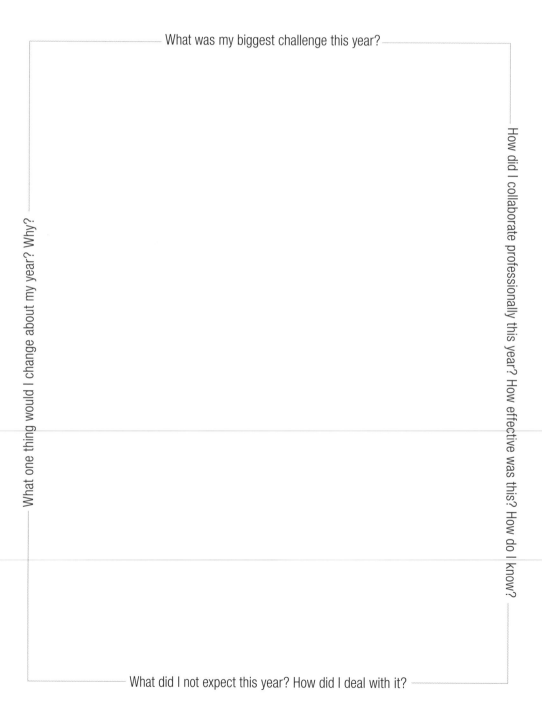

What was my biggest challenge this year?

How did I collaborate professionally this year? How effective was this? How do I know?

What one thing would I change about my year? Why?

What did I not expect this year? How did I deal with it?

How will next year benefit from your experiences this year?

What will I do differently next year?

Knowing what I know now, what advice would I have given myself on the first day of school? Will it apply next year?

What can I do to find valuable professional development next year?

How will I work to collaborate next year?

As you consider the story you want to tell about your year, choose evidence that will help an evaluator see that story in action. Following are some suggestions.

Evidence to Show Your Strengths in Planning and in Tailoring Your Instruction to Your Students

☐ lesson plans with evidence of reflections or notes on what you changed as well as written analysis of what did and did not work in the lesson

☐ assessments, unit plans, or assignments that reflect revisions with notes on why and how you changed them, how effective these changes were, and what you'll do next time

☐ student work samples that show the range of assignments your students completed along with scoring criteria, checklists, or rubrics

☐ evidence or notes of how your plans incorporated required benchmarks or standards as well as how they followed curriculum guidelines

☐ samples of your formative assessments, including facilitation grids, conference notes, anecdotal records, exit/entrance tickets, and quizzes, along with your reflections on how you used this information to inform instruction

☐ samples of summative assessments and projects, including directions, student work samples, rubrics, grading sheets with feedback, and your reflections on the unit and assessment, including changes for subsequent learning

☐ charts or documentation of student achievement and growth, whether standards-based or skill-based, as required by your district and evaluation model

☐ notes on curriculum mapping, instructional calendars you created, and other evidence of planning

☐ examples of your feedback to students

☐ samples or documentation of outside resources used in instruction, including field trips (and how they connected to learning in the classroom), guest speakers, and Skype visits

☐ artifacts showing how you used technology, including photos or screenshots if needed

Evidence to Show That You Are Attuned to Students' Needs

☐ differentiated assignments designed to meet student needs

☐ notes and evidence such as assignments or plans showing how you incorporated your knowledge of students and their families and cultures into your teaching

☐ student data such as pre- and postassessments, standardized test scores, benchmark assessments, and needs surveys from students, parents, and community used to inform instruction and planning, including plans or assignments noting how you used that information

☐ samples of plans that show lesson adjustments due to pacing or student needs

☐ documentation of student growth objectives, if required

☐ samples of letters of recommendation or log of recommendations given for students

☐ photos of bulletin boards of student work or student-created projects

Evidence to Show How You Involve Families and How You Are Active in the Students' Communities

☐ parent contact or community intervention logs, documenting the range of ways you informed parents and guardians and/or consulted with other professionals to provide student support, as well as samples such as classroom newsletters or blog posts, including those generated by students to keep families up-to-date

☐ notes and emails from parents, colleagues, and administrators that show your collegiality, professionalism, and responsiveness to student needs

☐ documentation of attendance and/or participation in school, district, and community events

Evidence to Show You Are a Collaborative Professional

☐ notes from department and faculty meetings, as well as notes from any informal meetings with colleagues, such as conversations over assessments or projects

☐ minutes or notes from any committees, PLCs, or other organized groups such as lesson-study or book-study groups

☐ evidence and samples of coplanning

☐ samples or evidence of collegial sharing, such as plans, units, online resources, and journals articles, and evidence of how they were used, if available

Evidence to Show Your Professional Growth Across the Year

- ☐ certificates of attendance and notes for any conferences or workshops you attended, along with evidence of how you applied your learning, including lesson plans, reflective journal entries, student work samples, assignment sheets, or rubrics

- ☐ evaluations from workshops, presentations, or trainings given, along with handouts, any teacher or stakeholder artifacts created, and examples of how the information was used afterward, if possible

- ☐ notes from a mentorship, including issues discussed

- ☐ professional and/or personal growth plan with notes on how you implemented it, what activities you did, how teacher goals and learning impacted student learning, and reflections on effectiveness and next steps

- ☐ documentation of action research you conducted

Evidence to Show You Are a Leader, Innovator, or Cutting-Edge Practitioner

- ☐ notes from mentoring of new teachers or supervision of fieldwork students

- ☐ notes from mentoring colleagues, including issues you discussed

- ☐ articles, blog posts, transcripts of social media chats, and other evidence of publishing or sharing your work and research

- ☐ documentation and artifacts from professional organizations you belong to, such as conference notes and agendas

- ☐ evidence of leadership activities such as organizing study groups, chairing committees, or implementing new initiatives or school service projects

Evidence to Show That You Are Keeping Clear Records

- ☐ grade book and attendance records

- ☐ samples of noninstructional records you kept, such as signed parent contracts, permission slips, and textbook distribution

- ☐ evidence of student-driven records and systems for student-centered classrooms

References

Accomplished California Teachers. 2015. "A Coherent System of Teacher Evaluation for Quality Teaching." *Education Policy Analysis Archives* 23 (17). http://dx.doi.org/10.14507/epaa.v23.2006.

Aguilar, Carla E., and Lauren Kapalka Richerme. 2014. "What Is Everyone Saying About Teacher Evaluation? Framing the Intended and Inadvertent Causes and Consequences of Race to the Top." *Arts Education Policy Review* 115 (4): 110–20. Professional Development Collection, EBSCOhost. doi:10.1080 /10632913.2014.947908.

Baker, Bruce D. 2013. "Gates Still Doesn't Get It! Trapped in a World of Circular Reasoning and Flawed Frameworks." *School Finance 101* (blog), January 9. https://schoolfinance101.wordpress.com/2013/01/09/gates-still-doesnt-get-it -trapped-in-a-world-of-circular-reasoning-flawed-frameworks/.

Baker, Bruce D., Joseph Oluwole, and Preston C. Green III. 2013. "The Legal Consequences of Mandating High Stakes Decisions Based on Low Quality Information: Teacher Evaluation in the Race-to-the-Top Era." *Education Policy Analysis Archives* 21 (5). http://epaa.asu.edu/ojs/article/view/1298.

Baker, Bruce D., and Mark Weber. 2016. *Deconstructing the Myth of American Public Schooling Inefficiency.* Washington, DC: Albert Shanker Institute. www.shankerinstitute.org/sites/shanker/files/Baker%20Weber%202016 %20Final.pdf.

Burke, Jim. 2000. *Reading Reminders: Tools, Tips, and Techniques.* Portsmouth, NH: Boynton/Cook.

Callahan, Kathe, and Leila Sadeghi. 2015. "Teacher Perceptions of the Value of Teacher Evaluations: New Jersey's ACHIEVE NJ." *International Journal of Educational Leadership Preparation* 10 (1): 46–59. ERIC, EBSCOhost. www.eric.ed.gov/contentdelivery/servlet/ERICServlet?accno=EJ1060978.

Carnegie Forum on Education and the Economy, Task Force on Teaching as a Profession. 1986. *A Nation Prepared: Teachers for the 21st Century: The Report of the Task Force on Teaching as a Profession.* Washington, DC: Carnegie Forum on Education and the Economy, Task Force on Teaching as a Profession. ERIC, EBSCOhost. https://eric.ed.gov/?id=ED268120.

Coleman, James S., Ernest Q. Campbell, Carol J. Hobson, James McPartland, Alexander M. Mood, Frederic D. Weinfeld, and Robert L. York. 1966. *Equality of Educational Opportunity*. Washington, DC: US Department of Health, Education, and Welfare, Office of Education. ERIC. https://eric.ed.gov/?id =ED012275.

Corbett, Dick, and Bruce Wilson. 2002. "What Urban Students Say About Good Teaching." *Educational Leadership* 60 (1): 18–22. www.ascd.org/publications /educational-leadership/sept02/vol60/num01/What-Urban-Students-Say-About -Good-Teaching.aspx.

Danielson, Charlotte. 2011. *The Framework for Teaching Evaluation Instrument, 2011 Edition*. Princeton, NJ: Danielson Group. http://sde.ok.gov/sde/sites /ok.gov.sde/files/TLE-DanielsonFramework.pdf.

———. 2013. *The Framework for Teaching Evaluation Instrument, 2013 Edition*. Princeton, NJ: Danielson Group. www.loccsd.ca/~div15/wp-content /uploads/2015/09/2013-framework-for-teaching-evaluation-instrument.pdf.

———. 2016. "Charlotte Danielson on Rethinking Teacher Evaluation." *EdWeek*, April 18. www.edweek.org/ew/articles/2016/04/20/charlotte-danielson-on -rethinking-teacher-evaluation.html.

Darling-Hammond, Linda, Audrey Amrein-Beardsley, Edward Haertel, and Jesse Rothstein. 2012. "Evaluating Teacher Evaluation." *Phi Delta Kappan* 93 (6): 8–15. Academic Search Premier, EBSCOhost.

Dewey, John. 1910. *How We Think*. New York: DC Heath.

Doherty, Kathryn M., and Sandi Jacobs. 2015. *State of the States 2015: Evaluating, Teaching, Leading, and Learning*. Washington, DC: National Council on Teacher Quality. www.nctq.org/dmsView/StateofStates2015.

Duhigg, Charles. 2014. *The Power of Habit: Why We Do What We Do in Life and Business*. New York: Random House Trade Paperbacks.

"Excerpts from the Carnegie Report on Teaching." 1986. *New York Times*, May 16. www.nytimes.com/1986/05/16/us/excerpts-from-the-carnegie-report-on -teaching.html?pagewanted=all.

Fullan, Michael. 1993. *Change Forces: Probing the Depths of Educational Reform*. Bristol, PA: Falmer. ERIC. http://files.eric.ed.gov/fulltext/ED373391.pdf.

Goldstein, Dana. 2014. *The Teacher Wars: A History of America's Most Embattled Profession*. New York: Doubleday.

Goodwin, Deborah and Mary Ann Webb. 2014. "Comparing Teachers' Paradigms with the Teaching and Learning Paradigm of Their State's Teacher Evaluation System." *Research in Higher Education Journal* 25 (Sept.): 1-11. ERIC. https://eric.ed.gov/?id=EJ1055341.

Graves, Donald H. 2001. *The Energy to Teach.* Portsmouth, NH: Heinemann.

Greene, Jay P. 2012. "Best Practices Are the Worst." *EducationNext* 12 (3): 72–73. http://educationnext.org/best-practices-are-the-worst/.

Hattie, John A. C. 2009. *Visible Learning: A Guide to Over 800 Meta-Analyses Relating to Achievement.* New York: Routledge.

Hewitt, Kimberly Kappler. 2015. "Educator Evaluation Policy That Incorporates EVAAS Value-Added Measures: Undermined Intentions and Exacerbated Inequities." *Education Policy Analysis Archives* 23 (76). http://dx.doi.org/10.14507/epaa.v23.1968.

Hunter, Madeline. 1985. "What's Wrong with Madeline Hunter?" *Educational Leadership* Feb.: 57-60. http://www.ascd.org/ASCD/pdf/journals/ed_lead/el_198502_hunter.pdf

Ingersoll, Richard M., Lisa Merrill, and Henry May. 2016. "Do Accountability Policies Push Teachers Out? Sanctions Exacerbate the Teacher Turnover Problem in Low-Performing Schools—but Giving Teachers More Classroom Autonomy Can Help Stem the Flood." *Educational Leadership* 73 (8): 44–49. Academic Search Premier, EBSCOhost. http://search.ebscohost.com/login.aspx?direct=true&AuthType=ip,cpid&custid=cjrlc155&db=aph&AN=115591948&site=ehost-live

Kittle, Penny. 2008. *Write Beside Them: Risk, Voice, and Clarity in High School Writing.* Portsmouth, NH: Heinemann.

Kittle, Penny. 2012. *Book Love: Developing Depth, Stamina, and Passion in Adolescent Readers.* Portsmouth, NH: Heinemann.

Lacireno-Paquet, Natalie, Claire Morgan, and Daniel Mello. 2014. "How States Use Student Learning Objectives in Teacher Evaluation Systems: A Review of State Websites." REL 2014–013. Washington, DC: US Department of Education, Institute of Education Sciences, National Center for Education Evaluation and Regional Assistance, Regional Educational Laboratory Northeast and Islands. https://ies.ed.gov/ncee/edlabs/regions/northeast/pdf/REL_2014013.pdf.

Lahey, Jessica. 2015. *The Gift of Failure: How the Best Parents Learn to Let Go So Their Children Can Succeed.* New York: Harper.

Marzano, Robert J. 1998. *A Theory-Based Meta-Analysis of Research on Instruction.* Aurora, CO: Mid-Continent Regional Educational Lab. ERIC. www.eric .ed.gov/contentdelivery/servlet/ERICservlet?accno=ED427087.

———. 2013. *The Marzano Teacher Evaluation Model.* Marzano Research Laboratory. http://www.marzanoresearch.com/hrs/leadership-tools/marzano-teacher-evaluation-model

———. 2014. "Looking at the Bigger Picture with Dr. Robert Marzano: Teacher Evaluation and Development for Improved Student Learning." Interviewed by Angela E. Quinn. *Delta Kappa Gamma Bulletin* 81 (1): 12–18. Academic Search Premier, EBSCOhost. http://web.a.ebscohost.com/ehost/pdfviewer /pdfviewer?sid=352e9acd-1dcf-4f82-959f-36c3cdfb929f%40sessionmgr4010&vi d=48&hid=4214.

———. 2017. *The Marzano Teacher Evaluation Model.* 2014 Protocol. Learning Sciences International. http://www.marzanocenter.com/teacher-evaluation /focused-model/.

———. 2017. *The Marzano Focused Teacher Evaluation Model.* Learning Sciences International. http://www.marzanocenter.com/teacher-evaluation/.

Marzano, Robert J., Barbara B. Gaddy, and Ceri Dean. 2000. *What Works in Classroom Instruction.* Aurora, CO: Mid-continent Regional Educational Lab. ERIC. https://eric.ed.gov/?id=ED468434.

Marzano, Robert J., Debra J. Pickering, and Jane E. Pollock. 2001. *Classroom Instruction That Works: Research-Based Strategies for Increasing Student Achievement.* Alexandria, VA: Association for Supervision and Curriculum Development.

MET Project. 2013. *Feedback for Better Teaching: Nine Principles for Using Measures of Effective Teaching.* Seattle: Bill and Melinda Gates Foundation. http:// k12education.gatesfoundation.org/wp-content/uploads/2015/05/MET_ Feedback-for-Better-Teaching_Principles-Paper.pdf.

Miller, Donalyn. 2009. *The Book Whisperer.* San Francisco: Jossey-Bass.

Mooney, John. 2012. "School Districts Comparison Shop for Teacher Evaluation Systems." *NJSpotlight*, October 17. www.njspotlight.com/stories/12/10/17 /school-districts-comparison-shop-for-teacher-evaluation-systems/.

Morgan, Grant B., Kari J. Hodge, Tonya M. Trepinski, and Lorin W. Anderson. 2014. "The Stability of Teacher Performance and Effectiveness: Implications for Policies Concerning Teacher Evaluation." *Education Policy Analysis Archives* 22

(95). ERIC, EBSCOhost. www.eric.ed.gov/contentdelivery/servlet /ERICServlet?accno=EJ1050120.

National Board for Professional Teaching Standards. 1989. *What Teachers Should Know and Be Able to Do.* Arlington, VA: National Board for Professional Teaching Standards. http://boardcertifiedteachers.org/sites/default/files/what_ teachers_should_know.pdf.

National Commission on Excellence in Education. 1983. *A Nation at Risk: The Imperative for Educational Reform: A Report to the Nation and the Secretary of Education, United States Department of Education.* Washington, DC: National Commission on Excellence in Education. www2.ed.gov/pubs /NatAtRisk/risk.html.

National Policy Board for Educational Administration. 2015. *Professional Standards for Educational Leaders 2015.* Reston, VA: National Policy Board for Educational Administration.

Perry, Bruce D. 2016. "The Brain Science Behind Student Trauma: Stress and Trauma Inhibit Students' Ability to Learn." *Education Week*, December 16. http://www.edweek.org/ew/articles/2016/12/14/the-brain-science-behind-student-trauma.html?r=413406031.

Provasnik, Stephen, Angelina KewalRamani, Mary McLaughlin Coleman, Lauren Gilbertson, Will Herring, and Qingshu Xie. 2007. *Status of Education in Rural America.* Washington, DC: National Center for Education Statistics. https://nces.ed.gov/pubsearch/pubsinfo.asp?pubid=2007040.

Ravitch, Diane. 2014. *Reign of Error: The Hoax of the Privatization Movement and the Danger to America's Public Schools.* New York: Vintage Books.

Riordan, Julie, Natalie Lacireno-Paquet, Karen Shakman, Candace Bocala, and Quincy Chang. 2015. *Redesigning Teacher Evaluation: Lessons from a Pilot Implementation.* REL 2015–030. Washington, DC: US Department of Education, Institute of Education Sciences, National Center for Education Evaluation and Regional Assistance, Regional Educational Laboratory Northeast and Islands. https://ies.ed.gov/ncee/edlabs/regions/northeast/pdf /REL_2015030.pdf.

Rodgers, Carol. 2002. "Defining Reflection: Another Look at John Dewey and Reflective Thinking." *Teachers College Record* 104 (4): 842–66. www.tcrecord .org/content.asp?contentid=10890. ID Number: 10890.

Ronfeldt, Matthew, Susanna Loeb, and James Wyckoff. 2012. *How Teacher Turnover Harms Student Achievement*. Working paper 70. Washington, DC: National Center for Analysis of Institutional Data in Education Research. www.caldercenter.org/sites/default/files/Ronfeldt-et-al.pdf.

Ruffini, Stephen J., Reino Makkonen, Jaclyn Tejwani, and MaryCruz Diaz. 2014. *Principal and Teacher Perceptions of Implementation of Multiple-Measure Teacher Evaluation Systems in Arizona*. REL 2015–062. Washington, DC: US Department of Education, Institute of Education Sciences, National Center for Education Evaluation and Regional Assistance, Regional Educational Laboratory West. https://ies.ed.gov/ncee/edlabs/regions/west/pdf/REL_2015062.pdf.

Santoro, Doris A. 2011. "Good Teaching in Difficult Times: Demoralization in the Pursuit of Good Work." *American Journal of Education* 118 (1): 1–23. doi:10.1086/662010.

Schmoker, Mike. 2012. "Why Complex Teacher Evaluations Don't Work." *EdWeek*, August 29. www.edweek.org/ew/articles/2012/08/29/02schmoker_ep.h32.html.

Schön, Donald A. 1983. *The Reflective Practitioner: How Professionals Think in Action*. New York: Basic Books.

Snook, Ivan, John O'Neill, John Clar, Anne-Marie O'Neill, and Roger Openshaw. 2009. "Invisible Learnings? A Commentary on John Hattie's book: *Visible Learning: A Synthesis of over 800 Meta-Analyses Relating to Achievement*." *New Zealand Journal of Educational Studies* 44 (1): 93–106. Academic Search Premier, EBSCOhost. AN 45447992.

Strauss, Valerie. 2015. "Bill Gates Keeps Pushing Common Core, with Big Money (and a Bid to Get Charles Koch to Like It)." *Washington Post*, December 27. www.washingtonpost.com/news/answer-sheet/wp/2015/12/27/bill-gates-keeps-pushing-common-core-with-big-money-and-a-bid-to-get-charles-koch-to-like-it/?utm_term=.f892248783ec.

Stronge and Associates. 2016. *Stronge Teacher Effectiveness Performance Evaluation System Performance Standards*. Williamsburg, VA: Stronge. https://www.strongeandassociates.com/files/components/Stronge+TEPES%20standards-for%20review.pdf.

———. 2017. "Stronge Effectiveness Performance Evaluation System." www.strongeandassociates.com/evaluating.html.

Terhart, Ewald. 2011. "Has John Hattie Really Found the Holy Grail of Research on Teaching? An Extended Review of *Visible Learning.*" *Journal of Curriculum Studies* 43 (3): 425–38. ERIC, EBSCOhost. doi:10.1080/00220272.2011.576774.

Tovani, Cris. 2000. *Do I Really Have to Teach Reading? Content Comprehension, Grades 6–12.* Portland, ME: Stenhouse.

———. 2011. *So What Do They Really Know? Assessment That Informs Teaching and Learning.* Portland, ME: Stenhouse.

Tucker, Marc, ed. 2011. *Surpassing Shanghai: An Agenda for American Education Built on the World's Leading Systems.* Cambridge, MA: Harvard Education Press.

Weisberg, Daniel, Susan Sexton, Jennifer Mulhern, and David Keeling with Joan Schunck, Ann Palcisco, and Kelli Morgan. 2009. *The Widget Effect: Our National Failure to Acknowledge and Act on Differences in Teacher Effectiveness.* 2nd ed. Brooklyn: New Teacher Project. http://tntp.org/assets/documents /TheWidgetEffect_2nd_ed.pdf.

Wiggins, Grant, and Jay McTighe. 2005. *Understanding by Design.* Expanded 2nd ed. Alexandria, VA: Association for Supervision and Curriculum Development.

Wilhelm, Jeffrey D. 1996. *You Gotta BE the Book: Teaching Engaged and Reflective Reading with Adolescents.* New York: Teachers College Press.

Williams, Jean. 2009. *McREL's Teacher Evaluation System.* Denver: McREL. www.medford.k12.nj.us/cms/lib/NJ01001377/Centricity/Domain/3 /McRELTeacher%20Evaluation%20Users%20Guide.pdf.

Zwiers, Jeff and Marie Crawford. 2011. *Academic Conversations: Classroom Talk That Fosters Critical Thinking and Content Understandings.* Portland, ME: Stenhouse.